I0605963

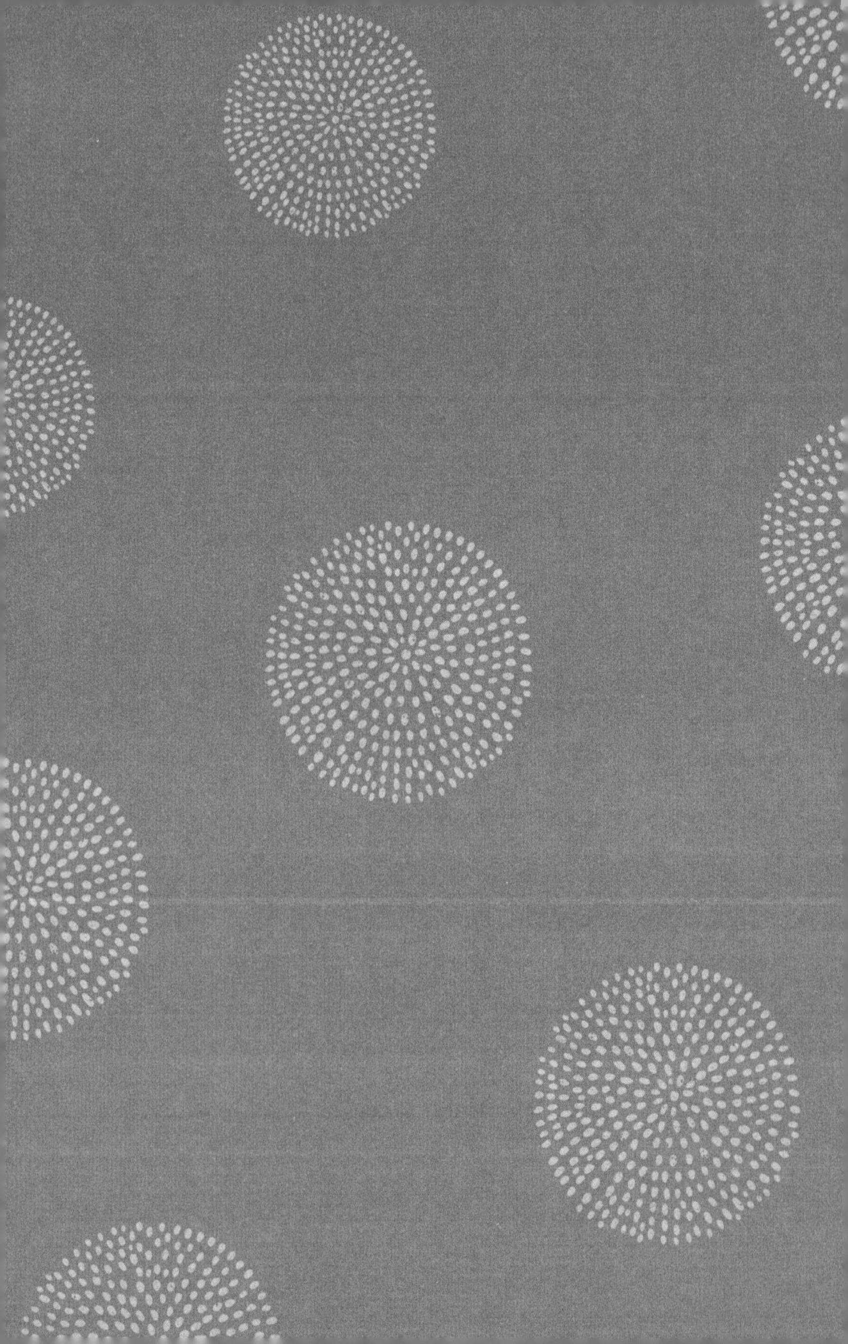

TO:

FROM:

DATE:

Coffee
& Jesus

A ROBUST BLEND OF

UPLIFTING DEVOTIONS +

PRAYERS FOR WOMEN

YOU are the reason we do what we do here at Barbour Publishing. We promise that we will always use our God-given talents to produce content with you in mind—and that we will remain biblically faithful, no matter what.

Thank you for being the heart of our business.

Print ISBN 979-8-89151-252-8

Cover design by Greg Jackson, Thinkpen Design

Published by Barbour Publishing, Inc., 1810 Barbour Drive, Uhrichsville, Ohio 44683, www.barbourbooks.com

Our mission is to inspire the world with the life-changing message of the Bible.

Printed in China.

INTRODUCTION

Morning coffee is a ritual many women enjoy. There is something peaceful and comforting about wrapping your hands around a warm mug of coffee before you begin each day. But what if there were more to this ritual? What if it deepened your faith and brought you closer to Jesus?

As Christians, we know that life's journey isn't only about mountaintop moments; it's also about hills and valleys. It's about challenges, successes, failures, celebrations, ordinary moments, and simple things. In daily rituals, like sipping a cup of coffee, we can find glimpses of Jesus' presence and love. So whether you're a coffee connoisseur or just a casual fan, we invite you to pour a cup and spend a few moments each day reading *Coffee & Jesus* and reflecting on its scriptures, devotions, and prayers. May this devotional journey inspire you to brew a stronger faith and nourish your soul, one cup at a time.

[God,] if you wake me each morning with the sound of your loving voice, I'll go to sleep each night trusting in you.

Psalm 143:8 MSG

WAKE UP AND SMELL THE COFFEE!

"Awake, awake, Deborah!
Awake, awake, sing a song!"
JUDGES 5:12 NLV

Oh, the rich, warm scent of freshly brewed coffee! Its aroma beckons you to wake up, roll out of bed, and face the day. You shuffle into the kitchen and pour the steaming hot liquid into your favorite mug. The first taste awakens your senses. It perks you up and drains the grogginess left from sleep. Some people say they're no good without coffee. That first cup of joe gives them a jolt and a jumpstart. Johann Sebastian Bach said it best in his *Coffee Cantata*, "If. . .I can't drink my little cup of coffee. . .then I would be like [a] dried up piece of roast goat."[1]

Beginning each day with a cozy cup of coffee is a lovely routine, but something more is needed. In today's scripture, the prophetess Deborah sings a victory song after her army, the Israelites, has defeated the Canaanites. Bible scholars interpret Deborah's words "Awake, awake!" as summoning the awakening of God's Spirit within her. We all need that kind of spiritual awakening, and what better way to awaken the Spirit within than by starting each day with coffee and Jesus?

Oh, Lord! Awake, awake Your Spirit within me. Amen.

[1] Kate Steinbeck, "Coffee Cantata, BWV 211 Libretto in German and English," *Pan Harmonia*, March 14, 2023, https://panharmonia.org/2023/03/14/coffee-cantata-bwv-211-libretto-in-german-and-english/.

TASTE AND SEE

O taste and see that the Lord is good.
How happy is the man who trusts in Him!
PSALM 34:8 NLV

A good cup of coffee requires fresh filtered water, freshly ground beans, and a ratio of water to grounds that is just right. Professional coffee tasters, called "cuppers," judge coffee based on its flavor, body, aroma, acidity, and aftertaste. A good cup of coffee is well balanced with no single taste characteristic overwhelming another. If coffee isn't brewed right, it loses its balance—and that ruins the taste.

Psalm 34:8 says, "O taste and see that the Lord is good." A good relationship with Jesus is like a perfect cup of coffee. When we put our trust in Him, all the ingredients come together for a rich, satisfying, and well-balanced life. Jesus' goodness is the perfect blend of His character, His power, His holiness, and His love. When we believe He is trustworthy, Jesus pours His goodness into our hearts. The flavor is perfect, it never disappoints, and Christ's love for us will never grow cold. As you begin each morning with Jesus, take time to pray and ask Him to guide you all day long.

Dear Lord Jesus, I trust in Your goodness.
Bless me with confidence and strength as
You lead me through this day. Amen.

FRESHLY BREWED

It is of the Lord's mercies that we are not consumed, because his compassions fail not. They are new every morning: great is thy faithfulness.

LAMENTATIONS 3:22–23 KJV

Some days, we wake up to what remains of yesterday's coffee. There it is in the pot, cold and stale. We wouldn't think of drinking it. Instead, we dump it and start with fresh water and new grounds. Yesterday's coffee is like yesterday's problems. After a night's sleep, they remain. We can leave them there, muddy and bitter, or we can dump them and start fresh.

In Isaiah 43:18–19 (NLV), the Lord says, "Do not remember the things that have happened before. Do not think about the things of the past. See, I will do a new thing. It will begin happening now. Will you not know about it? I will even make a road in the wilderness, and rivers in the desert." Hold on to His words, memorize them, and speak them to yourself as you begin each day. His promises are for you. Forgct thc former things. Give yourself a fresh start. Our Lord is compassionate and good. His mercies are unfailing and new every morning. Oh, great is His faithfulness!

....

Lord, I will let go of yesterday's troubles and start fresh today, putting all my faith and trust in You. Amen.

THE DAILY GRIND

Christian brothers, keep your minds thinking about whatever is true, whatever is respected, whatever is right, whatever is pure, whatever can be loved, and whatever is well thought of. If there is anything good and worth giving thanks for, think about these things.

PHILIPPIANS 4:8 NLV

In a 2011 interview with the *Chicago Tribune*, Betty White said, "It's your outlook on life that counts. If you take yourself lightly and don't take yourself too seriously, pretty soon you can find the humor in our everyday lives. And sometimes, it can be a lifesaver."[2] These are wise words. We should add to them the words of the apostle Paul in Philippians 4:8.

We wake up most mornings to monotonous routines that send us plodding through our day, minds set on work, solving problems, and finding more problems. We can face the day feeling apprehensive and dreary, or we can think about what is true, respected, right, pure, loved, well thought of, good, and worth giving thanks for. Add a little lightness and humor, as Betty said, and we have a positive attitude to get us through the daily grind, like a lifesaver.

Dear Jesus, guide me through my daily routine. Help me maintain a positive attitude and find a little humor today. Amen.

---

[2] *Chicago Tribune*, "Betty White, Romance Coach," *Chicago Tribune*, August 23, 2021, https://www.chicagotribune.com/2011/05/04/betty-white-romance-coach/.

A KISS AND A PRAYER

Laban got up early in the morning and kissed his grandchildren and daughters. He prayed that good would come to them. Then Laban left and returned home.

Genesis 31:55 NLV

We live in a world of uncertainty. We don't know what each day might bring, and that leaves us feeling anxious. In the morning, we kiss our loved ones goodbye. We go about our day keeping our family always on our minds, hoping they are safe and well. Hope is good, but hope by itself does nothing. We need to back it up with prayer and faith in Jesus.

As you begin your day with a devotional, reading your Bible, and perhaps listening to worship music, allow plenty of time for prayer. Surrender your day to Jesus. He already knows what will happen, and He has a plan. Give Him your family. Pray for their safety and well-being. Submit everything to Jesus and trust in Him. Then, when you tell your loved ones goodbye, you will do so not just hoping but confident, knowing they are safe in the care of the Lord.

Jesus, I surrender this day to You, and I entrust to You the care of my loved ones. I feel at peace knowing You are with them. Amen.

A GIVING SPIRIT

"Give, and it will be given to you. You will have more than enough. It can be pushed down and shaken together and it will still run over as it is given to you. The way you give to others is the way you will receive in return."

LUKE 6:38 NLV

Brewing coffee in a French press requires placing the grounds into the cylinder, soaking them in hot water, waiting several minutes, and then using the plunger to press the grounds to the bottom. Pressing allows more oil from the beans to escape, adding flavor. By experimenting with the ratio of water to coffee grounds, you discover just the right amount to make full-bodied, rich coffee. The perfect blend comes from the amount of effort you are willing to give.

In Luke 6:38, Jesus describes a similar process for giving. We receive based on what we are willing to give. The more effort we put into our giving, the more full-bodied our lives become. When we give, God gives us even more to share with others. The pot never runs dry. Instead, it fills to overflowing.

Lord Jesus, increase my spirit of giving. Lead me to put in time and effort blessing others, giving willingly and unselfishly in ways that please You. Amen.

GET IT TO GO

"No man will be able to stand against you all the days of your life. I will be with you just as I have been with Moses. I will be faithful to you and will not leave you alone."

JOSHUA 1:5 NLV

She planned morning time with Jesus, but the dog threw up, her husband couldn't find his keys, and her son overslept and missed the school bus. She drove him to school, discovered she'd forgotten his lunch, went home to get it, delivered it, then was late getting to work. Sound familiar? Some mornings, life gets in the way of spending time with Jesus. It doesn't have to, though.

Plan for those days. Memorize scripture. Meditate on it. Pray about it. Then you'll have an abundance of scripture stored in your heart to take with you wherever you go. When you grab your travel mug filled with hot coffee, grab a devotional book too. Read it at lunch or during a break. Pray on the way to work and praise Jesus. Thank Him for blessing you and ask Him to guide you throughout the day. Did you miss your morning time with Jesus? No worries. With a little planning, you can get it to go.

Dear Jesus, wherever I go, You will go with me. Amen.

JESUS EVERY MORNING

For everything that is in the world does not come from the Father. The desires of our flesh and the things our eyes see and want and the pride of this life come from the world. The world and all its desires will pass away. But the man who obeys God and does what He wants done will live forever.

1 JOHN 2:16–17 NLV

Ellen's resolution to get up earlier to spend time with Jesus had fallen by the wayside, and it showed. "You sure are grumpy in the morning," her daughter complained. A wave of guilt rushed through Ellen as she realized she had prioritized life's problems and worldly distractions above spending time with Jesus. She vowed to do better.

Morning time with Jesus gives us an optimistic start to the day. It anchors our hearts to His and draws us nearer to Him. Talking with Him in the morning gives us a sense of direction for the day. Knowing He lives in our hearts gives us peace. Even when we don't make time for Jesus, He makes time for us. Whatever gets in the way of us spending time with Him, nothing at all will separate us from His love.

Lord Jesus, forgive me for not making You my first priority. Thank You for making me Yours. Amen.

HIS PLANS, NOT MINE

"For I know the plans I have for you," says the Lord, "plans for well-being and not for trouble, to give you a future and a hope."
JEREMIAH 29:11 NLV

We schedule our day, listing important tasks and appointments. We leave home ready to check off each item, but then, you guessed it, life gets in the way. Something unexpected happens. At day's end, we look at our lists again and dwell on what we didn't accomplish.

The day didn't go the way we wanted, but it went exactly as the Lord had planned. Jesus was with us all day long. He knew something unexpected would happen, and He knew He would lead us through it. Jesus knew we wouldn't accomplish all that we planned. He knew we would end the day feeling disappointed. But if we look back at the day, we discover that what was unexpected led us to help someone in need, or maybe it reminded us to keep a positive attitude when things went wrong. The reason might be obvious or hidden, but there was a purpose for that thing that threw off our schedule. If we look back at our day, we will find Jesus.

Jesus, this morning I submit my plans to You. Not my will be done, Lord, but Yours. Amen.

A SONG AND A PRAYER

Let the words of my mouth and the thoughts of my heart be pleasing in Your eyes, O Lord, my Rock and the One Who saves me.

PSALM 19:14 NLV

In the morning when I rise,
Give me Jesus.
(Refrain)
Give me Jesus,
Give me Jesus.
You may have all the rest,
Give me Jesus.[3]

What better way to begin your day than with a song? In the morning when you rise, sing to the Lord. Sing to Him as you prepare for the day. Choose your favorite worship song or make one up. The words don't have to be perfect and neither does your singing voice. Just sing.

End your worship time with David's prayer in Psalm 19:14: "Let the words of my mouth and the thoughts of my heart be pleasing in Your eyes, O Lord, my Rock and the One Who saves me." Let this prayer be a reminder to you to honor the Lord with your words and keep Him in your thoughts.

Lord, in the morning when I rise I will praise You. I will praise You all day long. Amen.

---

[3] "Give Me Jesus," Hymnary.org, accessed March 3, 2025, https://hymnary.org/text/in_the_morning_when_i_rise_in_the_morn#tune.

FILTER WITH A PURPOSE

Watch your talk! No bad words should be coming from your mouth. Say what is good. Your words should help others grow as Christians.

EPHESIANS 4:29 NLV

Most coffee brewing methods use a filter, but some, such as the French press and Turkish coffee, do not. Which method is better, filtered or unfiltered? It's a matter of choice. Filters trap oils, resulting in smoother coffee. They keep grounds from getting into your cup. Unfiltered coffee allows oils to escape, enhancing the coffee's flavor. A study released in 2020 in the *European Journal of Preventive Cardiology* suggests that filtered coffee is better for our health because unfiltered coffee contains compounds that can raise bad cholesterol.

In Ephesians 4:29, Paul speaks about filtering our talk. He says no bad words should come from our mouths. Our speech should build others up, not cut them down. As Christians, it is our duty to help others grow in their faith. The words we use have a purpose—they should set a good example. As you go about your day today, imagine your words flowing through a filter, extracting those that won't please Jesus. Use that image as a reminder to allow only words that honor Him to leave your lips.

Lord God, may every word that I speak today bring You praise. Amen.

TWO LAWS

Jesus said to him, "'You must love the Lord your God with all your heart and with all your soul and with all your mind.' This is the first and greatest of the Laws. The second is like it, 'You must love your neighbor as you love yourself.'"

MATTHEW 22:37–39 NLV

When asked, "Teacher, which one is the greatest of the Laws?" (Matthew 22:36), Jesus' answer came from Deuteronomy 6:5: "You must love the Lord your God with all your heart and with all your soul and with all your strength." Jesus added a second law, "You must love your neighbor as you love yourself."

Deuteronomy 6:6–7 says, "Keep these words in your heart. . . . Teach them to your children. Talk about them when you sit in your house and when you walk on the road and when you lie down and when you get up." Remembering the Lord's words and doing your best to follow them leads to brighter days. Your love for Him will guide you, and your love for others will encourage relationships filled with forgiveness, compassion, and caring.

Dear Jesus, lead me to love You more each day. Speak these laws to my heart every morning. Speak them again to me throughout the day. Amen.

REVENGE!

He has brought back their own sin upon them
and will destroy them for their wrong-doing.
The Lord our God will destroy them.
PSALM 94:23 NLV

She spent the entire drive to work dwelling on what her coworker had said about her. Now, sitting at her desk, she sipped coffee from the cafeteria vending machine and thought of her weak reaction to yesterday's false accusations. She was stronger than that! She should have stood up for herself. She wanted a do-over so she could tell her coworker what she *really* thought. She wanted revenge.

When someone deliberately treats us badly or unjustly, it's not easy to follow Jesus' command to love one another. Dwelling on the transgression and wishing for revenge fuels our anger, and when we allow anger to rule our emotions we feel separated from the Lord. He says in Deuteronomy 32:35, "It is Mine to punish when their foot makes a false step." If we remember to leave the punishing to Jesus, it opens our hearts to forgiveness and brings us a little nearer to loving one another.

Lord, help me to stop thinking about what they did to me. I release them to You to deal with as You please. Free me from my angry thoughts and replace them with thoughts of You. Amen.

THOSE FRUSTRATING TEEN YEARS

Let us then approach God's throne of grace with confidence, so that we may receive mercy and find grace to help us in our time of need.

HEBREWS 4:16 NIV

Think of a time in your teen years when you said or did something that hurt someone's feelings. During those years of growing, changing, and uncertainty, we all messed up. Whether intentional or not, our words and actions caused hurt. Looking back now, with maturity, maybe we feel somewhat guilty. It's not too late to confess our sins to God and ask for His mercy and grace. As Christians, we have confidence that when we seek Him, He will always meet us with forgiveness and love.

There isn't a parent on earth who hasn't dealt with their teens' shifting emotions. Their actions frustrate and their words sometimes hurt. As we teach our children right from wrong, we can also be an example of Christ's grace and mercy. The way we apply discipline can provide them with confidence that whatever mistakes they make, they can always approach us assured of our love. When we discipline with a Christlike heart, we are reflecting the heart of God.

Jesus, being a parent is frustrating sometimes. Help me to react to my child's transgressions the way You do, with forgiveness, mercy, grace, and love. Amen.

HIS ABUNDANT BLESSINGS

The Lord has done great things for us and we are glad.
Psalm 126:3 NLV

Maybe you prefer having your coffee in the afternoon or after dinner. There is no perfect time to settle in with a cup of joe, just as there is no perfect time to settle in with Jesus. When you seek Him, He will be waiting for you, ready to listen, teach, and bless you.

In your quiet time with Him today, reflect on your many blessings. Think about how you have grown in character as you have come to know Him better. What great lessons has He taught you? Consider the familiar things you take for granted: each breath and beat of your heart, the presence of family and friends, a warm place to live, and running water. List His greatest blessings, those times He gave you what you hoped for, rescued you from trouble, or provided for you in ways you couldn't have imagined. Little blessings, big blessings—abundant blessings! The Lord is so good! Praise Him today with a glad and grateful heart.

Dear Lord, my heart is filled with gladness as I think of the many ways You bless me. You are so good to me, and I am deeply grateful. Amen.

STEADFAST HOPE

Be happy in your hope. Do not give up when trouble comes. Do not let anything stop you from praying.

ROMANS 12:12 NLV

What do you hope for? Women just like you are praying this morning, making their requests known to God. Some pray with hope for their bodies or hearts to be healed, for their marriage to be saved, or their child to be set free from addiction.

Hope can be steadfast or fleeting. It wanes when trouble comes or when we decide God has already said no to what we've asked for. But steadfast hope never gives up. It is firmly rooted in faith, trust, and believing that the Lord's timing and His answers are perfect. Isaiah 40:31 says, "But they who wait upon the Lord will get new strength. They will rise up with wings like eagles. They will run and not get tired. They will walk and not become weak." Is there something you have been praying for? Have you thought of giving up? Pray for new strength. Be happy in hope and sure that the Lord will answer your prayers.

Dear Jesus, I am weary from asking. Please give me new strength and reinforce my hope. Make steadfast my faith and trust in You. Amen.

WHY, WHY, WHY?

Gideon said to him, "O sir, if the Lord is with us, why has all this happened to us? Where are all His powerful works which our fathers told us about?"

JUDGES 6:13 NLV

Thousands of years ago, Gideon asked, "Why, Lord? Why did this happen? Where are You?" We are still asking. We wake up to reports of wildfires ravaging neighborhoods, school shootings, an endless profusion of senseless crimes, and we ask, "Lord, why? You have the power to do anything at all, so why did You allow this to happen?"

The truth is we can't know why God doesn't intervene. In Isaiah 55:8 He says, "For My thoughts are not your thoughts, and My ways are not your ways." For some, His answer isn't good enough, and failing to accept it leads to less faith and more bitterness.

When bad things happen, instead of being angry and asking God why, we can focus on His love. We can ask Him to comfort us and to show us how we can use what happened to bring Him glory. Some of the greatest help organizations in the world were born out of tragedy.

Oh, Lord, instead of asking why, help me to ask how. How can I use this thing to bring about something good? Amen.

I WILL RISE

*Rejoice not against me, O mine enemy:
when I fall, I shall arise; when I sit in darkness,
the LORD shall be a light unto me.*

MICAH 7:8 KJV

When bad things happen, we can wallow in their ugliness, or we can rise above them. Satan rejoices when he makes us miserable. We can sit in the darkness and listen to his despicable laughter, or we can respond to him with strength, saying, "Oh, my enemy. When I fall, I will rise! When you bring me darkness, the Lord will be my light."

Maybe you made your coffee a little stronger this morning knowing it would boost your energy. Spending time with the Lord this morning will boost your strength. He will provide you with His power to face all your troubles. If you fall, He will help you to rise. The Lord will light your path today. So get rid of the ugliness! Rise above it. The Lord, your God, is your strength. Remember Psalm 121:1–2 (NLV): "I will lift up my eyes to the mountains. Where will my help come from? My help comes from the Lord, Who made heaven and earth."

Oh, Lord, with Your mighty power giving me strength, I will rise above my troubles. Amen.

IT'S ALL GOOD

We know that God makes all things work together for the good of those who love Him and are chosen to be a part of His plan.

ROMANS 8:28 NLV

Romans 8:28 is one of the most often quoted Bible verses, and one that causes some people to doubt. They can't see God's goodness in the worst tragedies. If they start to shift their focus away from the ugly parts, they will see neighbors helping neighbors to clear rubble after a storm, strangers offering lodging to those without a home, and friends bringing food and offering comfort after a death. We find goodness when we look for it. Nevertheless, it's hard to notice good when the tragedy is personal. It isn't as apparent when we are in the middle of a breakup or have lost a job and money is tight.

In Mitch Albom's novel *The Five People You Meet in Heaven*, the main character dies and goes to heaven, where he meets people who have greatly impacted his life or whose life he has greatly impacted. While the book is fictional, there is truth in the message that all things work together for good—sometimes, though, we won't know how until we get to heaven.

When I can't find the goodness, Lord, I will still trust in You. Amen.

THE ONE WHO HUNG THE STARS

"He alone spreads out the heavens and walks up on the waves of the sea. He makes the Bear, Orion and the Pleiades and the stars of the south."

JOB 9:8–9 NLV

Serenity is sitting by a campfire at night and gazing up at the starry sky. The Bear, Orion, and the Pleiades are all there, just as they were in Job's time. The moon, the planets, star upon star upon star, as far as we can see. Beyond is a universe we can only imagine. The same God who hung the stars and created the universe made you. He made you with His love, a love that will last forever.

Paul wrote in Romans 8:38–39, "For I know that nothing can keep us from the love of God. Death cannot! Life cannot! Angels cannot! Leaders cannot! Any other power cannot! Hard things now or in the future cannot! The world above or the world below cannot! Any other living thing cannot keep us away from the love of God which is ours through Christ Jesus our Lord."

Tonight, go outside and look up at the stars. Behold the glory of God and remember how much He loves you.

Lord God, thank You for the promise of Your never-ending love. Amen.

WHEN I AM WEAK

I receive joy when I am weak. I receive joy when people talk against me and make it hard for me and try to hurt me and make trouble for me. I receive joy when all these things come to me because of Christ. For when I am weak, then I am strong.

2 Corinthians 12:10 NLV

Paul's words in 2 Corinthians 12:10 come after a litany of his troubles. He had been whipped, beaten, stoned, shipwrecked, and imprisoned. He faced danger everywhere he went because he continued to preach the gospel of Jesus and God's plan of salvation. Paul had been hungry, cold, tired, and now, as he sat in prison, he was in constant pain. Still, he wrote, "When I am weak, then I am strong."

Paul had found the key to building up extraordinary emotional strength. The weaker he became, the more he needed Jesus. His need for Jesus increased his faith, and his faith made Paul strong. He even found joy in his troubles because they led him nearer to Christ.

Are you facing troubles today? Bring them to Jesus. Put all your faith in Him. In your weakness, He will make you strong.

Dear Jesus, with faith I am able to endure whatever troubles I encounter. In my weakness, You give me strength. Amen.

COFFEE TALK

So when the name of Jesus is spoken, everyone in heaven and on earth and under the earth will bow down before Him. And every tongue will say Jesus Christ is Lord. Everyone will give honor to God the Father.

PHILIPPIANS 2:10–11 NLV

"Jesus, this coffee is awesome," said Valerie. She and her sister, Jan, were tasting a new brew in their favorite coffee shop.

Knowing Valerie's words weren't a prayer, Jan said, "Amen."

"What did you say?" Valerie inquired.

"I just said 'amen' to finish your prayer," Jan answered.

"But I didn't pray," Valerie said.

For Christians, it's frustrating to hear the Lord's name used in a bad way. We hear it in conversations, movies, television shows, and song lyrics. Using His name in vain has become part of our society's vernacular. Even some believers do it, forgetting that the third of God's Ten Commandments is "Thou shalt not take the name of the LORD thy God in vain: for the LORD will not hold him guiltless that taketh his name in vain" (Deuteronomy 5:11 KJV). Whether it's cursing or using His name as an exclamation, the Lord hears, and He dislikes it.

Lord God, Your name is holy and above all other names. It deserves honor and my deepest respect. Amen.

WEAK COFFEE, WEAK FAITH

If there is someone whose faith is weak, be kind and receive him. Do not argue about what he thinks.

ROMANS 14:1 NLV

"This coffee is weak," said Katie, pouring a small container of cream into her restaurant coffee. "How is your daughter? Any signs that her cancer is improving?"

Her friend poured cream into her own cup. "She had a scan last week. It showed the cancer has spread."

"Oh, I'm so sorry," Katie sympathized. "We'll keep praying. God is good."

"I've given up on God," her friend answered. "I don't pray anymore."

Katie could have responded with a lecture about weak faith, but she didn't. She knew in her friend's state of mind it wouldn't help her feel better. The time wasn't right for a deep talk about faith. Ecclesiastes 3:7 says, "There is. . .a time to be quiet, and a time to speak." Katie recalled those words and acted accordingly. Instead of saying, "Don't give up on God!" or "Never stop praying," Katie responded to her friend's weak faith with gentle kindness.

If you know someone who is experiencing a time of weak faith, pray for them. Ask God to strengthen them and show you how you can help.

Jesus, please strengthen my friend's faith and give her peace. Amen.

DIFFICULT THINGS

I can do all things because Christ gives me the strength.

PHILIPPIANS 4:13 NLV

What is the most difficult thing you have done? Did you complete a marathon, end a relationship, or survive cancer? Some goals we plan for, like when we train for a marathon. Others come by necessity. It's the necessary goals that are most difficult to accomplish. It takes a great deal of emotional strength to end a relationship or to navigate a life-changing disease. In situations like those, we need support from family, friends and—most of all—Jesus.

In John 16:33 Jesus said, "In the world you will have much trouble. But take hope! I have power over the world!" Some goals in life seem unattainable, but our Lord gives us strength to push through. We move forward, clinging to the promise that His plans for us are good. We trust that He knows what's ahead and He has power over it. If we have faith, Jesus lights the way. Without faith we slip into darkness.

When you face a difficult challenge, don't give up! Seek the support you need and believe with all your heart that Jesus will be your strength.

Dear Jesus, I need You! Be the light in my darkness and give me strength. Amen.

JESUS, MY FRIEND

The Lord spoke to Moses face to face,
as a man speaks to his friend.
EXODUS **33:11** NLV

When Moses encountered God in the burning bush, Moses hid his face and was afraid to look at Him. The Lord spoke to Moses as if he were a trusted friend, saying in Exodus 3:10 (NIV), "I am sending you to Pharaoh to bring my people the Israelites out of Egypt."

Moses lacked confidence and fear made him speak up, begging God to send someone else. Moses' relationship with God evolved. Instead of hiding his face, fearful of Him, Moses began building a trusting friendship with the Lord in which he wasn't afraid to speak his mind and ask questions. They had many conversations as Moses led the Israelites to the promised land. Their conversations strengthened Moses' trust in God and gave him confidence to become a great leader.

Moses' relationship with God is an example that our conversations with Him should be respectful but not fearful. The Lord is our friend. We can tell Him everything, question Him, and even ask Him to change His mind. He will always respond with love and forgive our transgressions.

Lord God, my friendship with You is a precious gift that grows stronger day by day. Thank You for listening to me, talking with me, and guiding me. Amen.

JOSEPH SCRIVEN

Answer me when I call, O my God Who is right and good! You have made a way for me when I needed help. Be kind to me, and hear my prayer.

PSALM 4:1 NLV

Joseph M. Scriven was a Canadian poet whose life was one of faith and also profound sadness. On the eve of his wedding, his fiancé fell from her horse while crossing a bridge. Joseph found her body drowned in the river. He trusted God to heal his broken heart by serving God and helping others. Joseph fell in love again, but tragedy struck once more when his second fiancé died of pneumonia. Later in life, he struggled with health issues, but through it all, Scriven never lost his faith. Instead, he wrote lyrics to the hymn "What a Friend We Have in Jesus":

What a friend we have in Jesus,
All our sins and griefs to bear!
What a privilege to carry
Everything to God in prayer!

His friendship with Jesus was the one constant throughout a life filled with tragedy. Joseph Scriven never stopped serving and relying on his friend. He died destitute, living in the homes of others, and still helping however he could.

Dear Jesus, in times of trouble, Your friendship is my comfort and my strength. Amen.

THE WAY

I have chosen the way of truth:
thy judgments have I laid before me.
PSALM 119:30 KJV

Latte, cappuccino, macchiato, flavored, decaffeinated. . . When it comes to coffee, we have so many choices. We sample each and decide which we find good and which are not to our liking. Finally, we land on the one we prefer.

Life is like that—so many choices. As we grow in maturity, we look back and see which choices were bad and which were good. The good choices led us closer to Jesus. When we followed His teachings and the example He set in the New Testament, we grew in our faith and learned to make better choices. As we continued to follow Him, we grew in trust, knowing that if we sought His guidance and obeyed, He would lead us to choose the right path. We learned to prefer Jesus over all others.

Jesus' way is not just the best way—it is the only way to rise above every obstacle. It is also the only way to heaven. In John 14:6 (NLV) He says, "I am the Way and the Truth and the Life. No one can go to the Father except by Me."

Dear Jesus, show me the way through life.
Guide me to make good choices that please You. Amen.

BAD ADVICE

In time of trouble, trusting in a man who is not faithful is like a bad tooth or a foot out of joint.

PROVERBS 25:19 NLV

Carol and her sister had different political ideologies. When they discussed politics, their tempers flared and they got into some nasty fights. When her sister joined a politically based group that Carol didn't agree with, Carol reached the end of her patience. She sought advice from a friend who shared her politics but not her faith in God.

"If she were my sister," said Carol's friend, "I would make her choose between me and that group. If she didn't choose me, then I'd stop speaking to her until she did." Carol took her friend's advice. It led to a terrible fight, and she didn't know if she and her sister would ever speak again. Had she looked to the Bible and Jesus for guidance, Carol might have discovered some peaceful and loving ways to deal with their conflict.

Whom do you trust for advice? It is wise to get counsel from someone who knows the Bible well and can guide you to Jesus' teachings. He has much to say about how to handle disagreements.

Lord Jesus, in times of trouble I will think before I act, and I will seek Your guidance. Amen.

BRIGHT, SHINING FACES

I looked for the Lord, and He answered me. And He took away all my fears. They looked to Him and their faces shined with joy. Their faces will never be ashamed.

PSALM 34:4–5 NLV

Oh, the joyful sounds of children playing without a care in the world. Running and laughing, their faces shining with joy. Maybe your best childhood memories are of playing happily with your friends. It was that innocent time before you walked the path of worldly concerns, grown-up fears, and shame for the mistakes you made.

In Psalm 34, David wrote of a time when he felt afraid. He had plenty to be afraid of. Jealous King Saul wanted David dead, forcing David to run for his life and go into hiding. But when David called on the Lord, He answered. He took away David's fears. David wrote that the faces of those who look to the Lord will shine with joy. They will never be ashamed.

When we trust in Him, we need not be afraid. When we confess our sins, He will forgive us, and we need not be ashamed. Jesus takes away our burdens and restores our innocence. He makes our faces shine with joy like happy children at play.

Oh, Lord, You are my redeemer. You are my joy. Amen.

WHO IS MY SHEPHERD?

"My people have been lost sheep. Their shepherds have led them the wrong way. They have made them turn away on the mountains. They have gone from mountain to hill and have forgotten their resting place."

JEREMIAH 50:6 NLV

While searching for something to replace the ugliness in her heart, Simone connected with a man who called himself Prophet Benjamin. He invited Simone to join their church community, and when she did, Simone was drawn into a cultish organization that worshipped a Jesus that was nothing like our Lord.

False teaching doesn't align with the Bible. The Lord warned us in Matthew 7:15, "Watch out for false teachers. They come to you dressed as if they were sheep. On the inside they are hungry wolves." Peter adds in 2 Peter 2:14–15, "They get weak people to go along with them. . . . They have left the right way and have gone the wrong way."

In John 10:27 Jesus said, "My sheep hear My voice and I know them. They follow Me." If teaching is contrary to what the Bible says, it is false teaching. Be careful. Don't allow false teachers to lead you away from the one true shepherd, Jesus.

Jesus, You are my only shepherd. Protect me from false teaching. Lead me down the path of righteousness. Amen.

PSALM 23

"I, even I, am He Who comforts you."
ISAIAH 51:12 NLV

Do you need comfort, encouragement, or strength? Then turn to the beloved words of Psalm 23:

> *The Lord is my Shepherd. I will have everything I need. He lets me rest in fields of green grass. He leads me beside the quiet waters. He makes me strong again. He leads me in the way of living right with Himself which brings honor to His name. Yes, even if I walk through the valley of the shadow of death, I will not be afraid of anything, because You are with me. You have a walking stick with which to guide and one with which to help. These comfort me. You are making a table of food ready for me in front of those who hate me. You have poured oil on my head. I have everything I need. For sure, You will give me goodness and loving-kindness all the days of my life. Then I will live with You in Your house forever.*

When you don't know how to pray, you can always pray the Twenty-Third Psalm. Its words are your assurance that Jesus is always with you and will forever meet your needs.

Dear Jesus, Your love sustains me. Thank You for being my always and my everything. Amen.

COFFEE WITH FRIENDS

And let us consider how we may spur one another on toward love and good deeds, not giving up meeting together, as some are in the habit of doing, but encouraging one another—and all the more as you see the Day approaching.

HEBREWS 10:24–25 NIV

What could be better than coffee with friends? Coffee with friends and Jesus! A cozy coffee shop is the perfect place to meet with Christian friends for Bible study or to discuss ways you can be disciples in your community.

Today's scripture reminds us not to give up on meeting with other believers. Fellowship reaches beyond the church. It's important to have a regular routine of being with Christian friends who encourage us in our faith, lift us up when we're down, and walk the road of life with us and Jesus.

If you aren't already doing so, plan to meet regularly with friends to have coffee with Jesus. Study the Bible together. Form a Christian book club to discuss faith-based novels. Plan outreach projects. In fellowship, you will strengthen your bond of friendship and also your faith in the Lord.

Jesus, lead me into routine fellowship with my Christian friends. Show us how we can work together to bring more of You to those in need. Amen.

ANGELS AMONG US

Do not forget to show hospitality to strangers, for by so doing some people have shown hospitality to angels without knowing it.

HEBREWS 13:2 NIV

Bonnie was volunteering at a center for the homeless when a man walked in from the street and shouted, "Repent! The day of the Lord is near. Jesus is the way to heaven!" His behavior was disruptive, and he was escorted out. As Bonnie served coffee and donuts to others there, a woman whispered to her, "Do you know what he meant, 'The day of the Lord is near'?" Bonnie sat with her and explained the gospel. By the end of their conversation, the woman had prayed and asked Jesus to come into her heart. Bonnie reached out with kindness and further helped the woman to get off the streets and begin a new life.

The Lord has His way of putting people in just the right place at the right time. The shouts of a disruptive stranger were the driving force that led this woman to accept Jesus as Lord and Savior. Bonnie was the one she needed for a fresh start. Angels are among us. Sometimes, they are ordinary people—just like you.

Lord, use me. Lead me to the ones You have chosen for me to help. Amen.

THE RECIPE

All the Holy Writings are God-given and are made alive by Him. Man is helped when he is taught God's Word. It shows what is wrong. It changes the way of a man's life. It shows him how to be right with God. It gives the man who belongs to God everything he needs to work well for Him.

2 Timothy 3:16–17 NLV

"Can you make a medium iced sweet and salty (extra sweet) and add hazelnut, toasted marshmallow, caramel, white chocolate drizzle, and cold foam?"

"I can!" answered the barista. She worked for a coffee shop that encouraged customers to make up their own recipes. She didn't require a recipe book. She was well trained in putting ingredients together to meet any request.

When we study the Bible and memorize its principles and words, we become somewhat like that barista. We can put its ingredients together to handle anything. The Bible is the recipe we need to get through life. Its words are God-given, and who better to train us than Him? Study the Bible. Meditate on its words. Then when someone asks, "Can you. . .?" you'll answer with confidence, "Yes, I can!"

Lord God, I will hold Your Word inside my heart. Be my Teacher. Make me able to say, "I can!" Amen.

DISCIPLES OF CHRIST

My Christian brothers, what good does it do if you say you have faith but do not do things that prove you have faith?

JAMES 2:14 NLV

What good is it if we read the Bible and don't put its words into action? That's what James asks in today's scripture verse. As believers, we are called to reflect God's Word in everything we say and do. If we say we believe but don't live our belief, then our words are empty. The Lord wants us to be His disciples, to share His words, and to be examples of what it means to live as Christians.

In the 1960s, a parish priest, Peter Scholtes, wrote a hymn titled "They'll Know We Are Christians by Our Love." It reminds us to be one in spirit and act as living examples of God's love. As disciples of Christ, it is our responsibility not only to say we believe in Jesus but to show we believe in Him through our actions and our words. Let His love shine through you today. Let God's words be on your lips.

Jesus, may I live as Your disciple, filled with purpose, always ready to share Your words and Your love. Amen.

MORE LIKE JESUS

But the fruit that comes from having the Holy Spirit in our lives is: love, joy, peace, not giving up, being kind, being good, having faith, being gentle, and being the boss over our own desires. The Law is not against these things.

GALATIANS 5:22–23 NLV

As you sit there today drinking your coffee and spending time with Jesus, think about what it means to reflect His character. In the verses above, Paul suggests nine character traits that reflect Jesus living inside our hearts. They are love, joy, peace, perseverance, kindness, goodness, faithfulness, gentleness, and self-control. These traits grow in us as we grow in our understanding of who Jesus is and how He interacted with others while here on earth.

Take an inventory of your own positive character traits. Are the nine in Paul's list among them? The Lord has blessed you with these traits so you can show others what it means to be His follower. Ask Jesus to help grow the fruits of the Spirit inside your heart. Pray that you will become more like Him.

Dear Lord Jesus, plant in my heart seeds of love, joy, peace, perseverance, kindness, goodness, faithfulness, gentleness, and self-control. Help me to nurture them so I will grow in character to become more like You. Amen.

CHOSEN

"You have not chosen Me. I have chosen you. I have set you apart for the work of bringing in fruit."
JOHN 15:16 NLV

God chose you. He chose to give you life. He chose to put you on earth with the purpose of serving Him. Your existence has nothing to do with *you*. It is only because of God that you are here. Whether you decide to serve Him is up to you. God won't force you to become His servant.

But if you do decide to serve Him, He expects you to bring in more fruit. In Mark 16:15 Jesus told His disciples, "You are to go to all the world and preach the Good News to every person." It was their purpose to gain more followers—to bring in more fruit. Throughout the early years of Christianity, men and women risked, and gave, their lives to fulfill the purpose of leading others to Christ. Today, Jesus is calling on you to be His follower and bring in the fruit. He said to His followers in Matthew 9:37, "There is much grain ready to gather. But the workmen are few."

What can you do, through your words and your deeds, to share the gospel and lead others to Christ?

My Lord, lead me to those who need to know You. Show me the way to guide them to You. Amen.

IN HIS ARMS

But I am calm and quiet, like a baby with its mother.
I am at peace, like a baby with its mother.

PSALM 131:2 NCV

Walking through a busy airport terminal, you might notice a young mother sitting and holding her sleeping baby. Amid all the chaos, the baby is at peace, calm and quiet, safely resting in its mother's arms.

Oh, that we could know that kind of peace in a world of chaos. We can! It comes with building a solid trust in the Lord. He promises to love, comfort, and protect us. He is our shelter in a storm, our resting place. When we believe with all our hearts that His power and strength will keep us safe, we can feel the warmth of His love surrounding us. We experience a sense of calm beyond our understanding.

Deuteronomy 33:27 tells us, "The God Who lives forever is your safe place. His arms are always under you." His strong but gentle arms wrap around you, hold you, and lift you up and out of trouble. Build your trust in Him. Ask Him to calm you and give you peace, like a baby with its mother.

Dear Jesus, be my peace. When I am worried or afraid, hold me in Your gentle arms and quiet me with Your love. Amen.

HE DOES THE IMPOSSIBLE

God is able to do much more than we ask or think through His power working in us.
EPHESIANS 3:20 NLV

The 1970s sitcom *Laverne & Shirley* followed the lives of two single women, best friends and roommates Laverne DeFazio and Shirley Feeney. Set in Milwaukee in the late 1950s, the young women pursued their hopes and dreams. The show's theme song reflected their positivity, willingness to take risks, overcome obstacles, and persevere. Laverne and Shirley had the attitude that nothing was impossible. Nothing would get in their way!

If we combine a positive attitude with faith in the Lord, nothing will get in *our* way, either. His power working through us allows us to accomplish much more than we ask or think. When we put our faith in Him, we will overcome the obstacles. If we become weary, He will give us strength to persevere.

Be like Laverne and Shirley. Don't allow anything to hold you back from pursuing your hopes and dreams. Talk with the Lord about it. He will help you to reach your goals. With Jesus leading your way, everything is possible.

Lord, I haven't told You some of my hopes and dreams because they seemed impossible. But with You, all things are possible! Let's talk about what I want to accomplish. Amen.

A GOOD LAND

For the LORD your God is bringing you into a good land—a land with brooks, streams, and deep springs gushing out into the valleys and hills.

DEUTERONOMY 8:7 NIV

Kelsey's husband and their two young children lay sleeping in their hotel room. Just before dawn, Kelsey sat in the only chair in the room, reading the Bible on her phone. Never could she ever have imagined that their house and all their belongings would be lost in a wildfire. "What next? What now?" she asked the Lord.

Kelsey searched randomly for encouraging scripture verses and landed on Deuteronomy 8:7. She knew it was God telling her that He would bring them through this difficult time. She prayed for renewal and decided to trust in His promises.

In times of trouble, we can trust our Lord to walk with us and lead us to "a good land." If we obey Him and follow Him, He will ease our pain, refresh us, and help us to put back together the broken pieces of our lives.

Maybe, like Kelsey, you need restoration. Put your faith and hope in Jesus. He will never let you down.

Lord, I need You. Restore me.
Lead me to the good land. Amen.

LORD, SEND ME

Then I heard the voice of the Lord, saying, "Whom should I send? Who will go for Us?" Then I said, "Here am I. Send me!"

Isaiah 6:8 NLV

God puts in all our hearts the ability to be courageous. For some, that character trait is center stage. These are the bold ones, the risk takers. When the Lord says, "Whom should I send?" they say, "Send me!" For many of us, though, our courageous trait lies dormant until we come face-to-face with danger. If you were in a crowd of onlookers seeing someone in desperate trouble, would you be the first to shout, "God, send me!"?

It takes an enormous amount of courage to risk our own lives, courage that comes only from the Lord. Hopefully, you will never be in a life-or-death situation. But if it were to happen, Jesus would be right there with you. He would say, "Here I am!"

In *The Screwtape Letters*, C. S. Lewis wrote, "Courage is not simply one of the virtues but the form of every virtue at the testing point."[4] If you were at that testing point, what would you do? Would you say, "Lord, send me"?

Here I am, Lord. Build up my courage. In the face of danger, please make me strong. Amen.

[4] C.S. Lewis, *The Screwtape Letters*, (Geoffrey Bles, the Centenary Press, 1944), https://gutenberg.ca/ebooks/lewiscs-screwtapeletters/lewiscs-screwtapeletters-00-h.html.

CHILDREN OF GOD

See what great love the Father has for us that He would call us His children. And that is what we are.

1 JOHN 3:1 NLV

"Mom! Don't embarrass me." Most kids go through phases when they don't want to be treated like children. "Don't hold my hand, mess with my hair, or call me your baby!" To dislike being treated like a child is part of growing up. It's hard for parents, though, to let go of little public displays of affection. No matter how old our children are, they remain our babies. Even though they dislike it in public, most kids still want to be held, hugged, and loved.

All of us are God's children, and we want to feel loved. David says in Psalm 71:18, "Even when I am old and my hair is turning white, O God, do not leave me alone." Our heavenly Father will never leave us. Throughout our lives, He will walk with us, hold our hands, protect us, comfort us, and—most of all—love us. Like our own children, we will go through phases when we push Him away. But just like us as parents, the Lord will never stop loving us. We will always be His babies.

Lord Jesus, I love being loved by You. Amen.

PEACEMAKERS

Blessed are the peacemakers: for they shall be called the children of God.
MATTHEW 5:9 KJV

We desire world peace, but we know that's not possible until Jesus returns and evil ends forever. Still, we can bring peace into our own little corners of the world. This prayer, often attributed to Francis of Assisi, suggests how we can do that:

Lord, make me an instrument of Thy peace.
Where there is hatred, let me sow love;
Where there is injury, pardon;
Where there is error, truth;
Where there is doubt, faith;
Where there is despair, hope;
Where there is darkness, light;
And where there is sadness, joy. . . .
Grant that I may not so much seek
To be consoled as to console;
To be understood as to understand;
To be loved as to love.[5]

Jesus said, "Blessed are the peacemakers." When we bring peace wherever we go, we demonstrate that we are children of God.

Lord, help me to bring peace into every situation. Amen.

---

[5] Christian Renoux, "The Origin of the Peace Prayer of St. Francis," *The Origin and Original Text of the Peace Prayer of St. Francis*, accessed March 3, 2025, https://www.franciscan-archive.org/franciscana/peace.html.

DRY TIMES

The Lord will always lead you. He will meet the needs of your soul in the dry times.

ISAIAH 58:11 NLV

Before their Bible study, Shana and her friend Karen stopped in the church hall to get a cup of coffee. "I don't know what's wrong with me," Karen confided. "I'm going through a time when I don't feel connected to Jesus."

"You're in a dry time," Shana told her. "It happens."

As Christians, it's not unusual to face times when prayer is hard, reading the Bible seems boring, and spending devotional time is challenging. It's a dry time, a time when Satan slips in and erects a wall between us and the Lord. When we notice our need for Jesus beginning to wane, it's time to get busy and tear down that wall.

At Bible study, Karen shared how she felt. A friend suggested she put faith ahead of feelings. Jesus hadn't left her—nor would He ever. Another reminded her of Psalm 51:12: "Let the joy of Your saving power return to me. And give me a willing spirit to obey you." As she pursued Jesus and asked for His help, Karen's passion for Him returned.

Dear Jesus, let the joy of loving You return to me, and give me a willing spirit. Amen.

ONE MISSING PIECE

GOD made my life complete when I placed all the pieces before him.
2 SAMUEL 22:21 MSG

After breaking his hip, Renae's elderly father recovered in a skilled nursing facility. Frustrated that he couldn't be active, he discovered that complicated jigsaw puzzles gave him something challenging to do. Renae brought him the most difficult puzzle she could find. It kept her dad busy for days.

Upon visiting him one afternoon, Renae found him sullen. "What's wrong?" she asked.

"It's that puzzle," he replied. "It was missing the last piece."

Some people work hard to overcome challenges and achieve their goals, but in the end, they discover that something is missing. They need one last piece that would make their lives complete. That missing piece is Jesus, and sadly, some people never find Him. When Jesus enters our hearts, then all the pieces of our lives come together, and we feel complete.

How does Jesus fit into the puzzle of your life? By adding Him sooner than later, you will find new hope, purpose, and a deep sense of fulfillment and relief.

Jesus, You make my life complete. If I place You first in my life, then all of the other pieces will come together exactly as You've planned. Amen.

SO LOVELY

The daughter of the King is beautiful within.
Her clothes are made with gold.

Psalm 45:13 NLV

Turn to social media and you'll find influencers promoting lipstick, concealer, foundation, and mascara. In your feeds, you will see countless ads for every kind of beauty product. Many people shopping for beauty products turn to social media influencers and online reviews for recommendations. The average American woman spends a healthy amount of her annual budget on beauty products.

As women, we want to look our best, but it's important to remember that true beauty comes from the inside. In 1 Samuel 16:7 the Lord said to Samuel, "A man looks at the outside of a person, but the Lord looks at the heart." Even with perfect makeup and the most fashionable clothes, you will never be as lovely on the outside as you are on the inside. You are not only a child of God, but you are also the daughter of the King of all kings. Come to Him, and He will clothe you in a gown of righteousness and give you a heart of gold.

Lord God, thank You for making me beautiful both inside and out. Amen.

A BAG FULL OF BURDENS

"For My way of carrying a load is easy and My load is not heavy."
MATTHEW 11:30 NLV

Linda was in a rush to get her groceries home and pick up her daughter at school. At the self-checkout, she grabbed just one paper bag. She squeezed all her groceries into it. Then, realizing it was heavy, she put the bag in a cart and hurried to her car. As she lifted the bag into the trunk, the weight of the items tore the bag, and everything spilled out onto the ground. Had she thought before she packed the bag so full, the mess wouldn't have happened.

Similarly, we can pack our lives so full of concerns that the load becomes too heavy to carry. If we don't lighten the load, we can end up with a mess. Jesus says, "My way of carrying a load is easy and My load is not heavy." So give Him your worries and concerns. He will carry them all and, at the same time, work with you to keep your burdens light.

Jesus, my Savior, take these worries and concerns I'm carrying. The load is too heavy for me to bear. Take them. Then lead me and guide me so my burden will be light. Amen.

THANKS A LATTE!

In everything give thanks. This is what God wants you to do because of Christ Jesus.

1 THESSALONIANS 5:18 NLV

At the drive-through on our way to work, we order our latte, mocha, or just plain coffee. When the associate hands us the cup, the words trip off our tongues, "Thanks. Have a nice day." It's easy to say thank you when we get what we want, but what if we were handed a half-full cup of liquid that bore no resemblance to coffee? Would we say thank you then? When we don't get what we want, it's hard to give thanks. If we lose a job, finances are tight, a loved one leaves us, or we become ill—are we thankful?

In his letter to the church in Thessalonica, Paul instructed its members to give thanks in all circumstances because that's what God wanted them to do. He reminded them of Jesus' sacrifice, giving His life for ours. Even in bad times, we can be grateful that we are alive and have the promise of eternal life in heaven. In good times and in bad, the Lord is always good. Thanks be to our Savior for His faithfulness and never-ending love.

Lord Jesus, in every circumstance, I am grateful that You are my friend and my Savior. Amen.

FOR SUCH A TIME AS THIS

"Who knows if you have not become queen for such a time as this?"

Esther 4:14 NLV

An evil plot was brewing to kill all the Jews, and the only one who could stop it was Queen Esther. It would be risky, but her cousin, Mordecai, encouraged her by saying, "Who knows if you have not become queen for such a time as this?"

The Bible says, "There is a special time for everything" (Ecclesiastes 3:1). God works in us and through us to fulfill His every purpose (Philippians 2:13). Just like Queen Esther, each of us has a purpose in life. What is it? Only God knows, but if we pray and ask, He will guide us.

None of us were born to wander aimlessly through life. We were born to serve the Lord. Do you feel Him leading you toward a specific purpose or goal? Don't ignore those feelings. Pray about them. It might not be apparent now, but perhaps in the future you will see how God led you where He wanted you to be. Each of us was born to lend a helping hand and further His kingdom here on earth.

Dear Jesus, what is my purpose? I am ready to be led wherever You want me to go. Amen.

WHAT SHALL I SAY?

"When you are put into their hands, do not worry what you will say or how you will say it. The words will be given you when the time comes. It will not be you who will speak the words. The Spirit of your Father will speak through you."

MATTHEW 10:19–20 NLV

Sometimes, we find ourselves at a loss for words. This happens a lot when something unexpected happens or when we need to comfort people in their time of need. We worry that our words won't be enough or right or that they might even make a situation worse.

When Jesus sent His disciples out into the world, He warned them they would face hard times. He told them not to worry about what to say or how to say it. In those difficult situations, the Holy Spirit would be their guide and give them the right words at the right times. Jesus' instructions still apply. When we can't find the words, we can say to ourselves, "Holy Spirit, help me," and then wait for Him to speak His words into our hearts. He is with us always, and He will never let us down.

Dear Lord, let Your Holy Spirit guide me and speak for me when I don't know what to say. Amen.

RETREAT OR ADVANCE?

"When you pass through the waters, I will be with you. When you pass through the rivers, they will not flow over you. When you walk through the fire, you will not be burned. The fire will not destroy you. For I am the Lord your God, the Holy One of Israel, Who saves you."

ISAIAH 43:2–3 NLV

In his 1933 inaugural address, President Franklin D. Roosevelt uttered these words that have been passed down through history: "Let me assert my firm belief that the only thing we have to fear is fear itself, nameless, unreasoning, unjustified terror which paralyzes needed efforts to convert retreat into advance."[6]

Imagine an army so frozen with fear that they will only retreat. It takes courage to face fear and keep moving forward. During Roosevelt's presidency, citizens faced a deep financial depression. Today, they face a different sort of depression brought on by a world filled with evil. In Roosevelt's time and in ours, God has been and continues to be our way through fear. Today's scripture reminds us of God's promise that nothing will destroy us if we put our faith in Him. He is the Lord our God, the Holy One who saves us.

Jesus, You have already conquered everything I fear. Help me not to feel afraid. Amen.

---

[6] "First Inaugural Address," FDR Presidential Library & Museum, accessed March 3, 2025, https://www.fdrlibrary.org/first-inaugural-curriculum-hub.

THANK GOD FOR YOU!

I thank God for you whenever I think of you.

PHILIPPIANS 1:3 NLV

Sandra was thirty-three when her mother died. Now in her mid-fifties, Sandra reflected on the thirty-three years her mom had been with her. She realized how much she had learned from her mother during those years. Her mother's wisdom had stayed with Sandra and carried her through the rough times. She was a better mom to her own kids by applying her mother's parenting techniques. Her mother had taught her grace and forgiveness, and—best of all—led Sandra to accept Jesus as her Savior. As she thought about her mother, Sandra whispered a scripture verse she had memorized long ago: "I thank God for you whenever I think of you."

The special people we remember are those who played a significant role in shaping us into the women we are today. We have inherited the examples they set and taken the lessons we learned from them into the future, incorporating the best of their qualities into our own lives.

Who are your special people? As you think of each one, thank the Lord for them.

Dear Lord, thank You for the special people You have put in my life. I am blessed by each and every one. Amen.

ON THIN ICE

The wise see danger ahead and avoid it,
but fools keep going and get into trouble.
PROVERBS 27:12 NCV

Ice fishing is a seasonal sport enjoyed by men and women who reside in the North. When inland lakes freeze over, they bring shanties onto the ice, drill holes, and set lines for panfish, trout, and pike. Those accustomed to ice fishing are wise about how thick the ice must be to support the weight of them walking on it, and also the weight of shanties and vehicles. Sometimes, an unexperienced person doesn't see the danger in thin ice, keeps going, and gets into trouble. Thank God for those who respond and come to that person's rescue.

Life can be a little like ice fishing. Those who have wisdom stop and think about whether danger lies ahead. If they perceive it, they avoid it. But those who don't think keep going and plunge into trouble. A foolish spirit wants what it wants and wants it now. Proverbs 27:12 warns against this. It encourages us to be cautious. Especially when we are curious or wanting to try something new, it is wise to stop, think, and be careful.

Dear Jesus, before I walk into the future,
remind me to be careful about where I step.
Give me wisdom wherever I go. Amen.

BLESSED TO GIVE

"In everything I did, I showed you that by this kind of hard work we must help the weak, remembering the words the Lord Jesus himself said: 'It is more blessed to give than to receive.'"

Acts 20:35 NIV

Jesus' words as quoted in Acts 20:35 are often repeated, even by those who don't know the Bible. "It is more blessed to give than to receive." The act of unselfish giving not only blesses others, but it blesses the giver as well. The more you are able to give, the more you can help the world. It feels good to help. Perhaps Susan B, Anthony said it best: "The older I get, the greater power I seem to have to help the world; I am like a snowball—the further I am rolled the more I gain."[7]

Ecclesiastes 11:1 says (KJV), "Cast thy bread upon the waters: for thou shalt find it after many days." What we give has a way of coming back to us, providing us with even more to give. You will find the Law of Reciprocity demonstrated many times in the Bible. We reap what we sow. The more seeds of helpfulness we sow, the greater the harvest. The greater the harvest the more people we can "feed."

Lord, what can I give today to help someone? Amen.

[7] Ida Husted Harper, ed, *The Life and Work of Susan B. Anthony: Including Public Addresses, Her Own Letters and Many from Her Contemporaries During Fifty Years* (Bowen-Merrill, 1898), 2.859.

THY WILL BE DONE

He said, "Father, if it can be done, take away what must happen to Me. Even so, not what I want, but what You want."

LUKE 22:42 NLV

Crystal and Ken's daughter, Anna, was born with physical disabilities. The doctors held little hope for her long-term survival, but by God's grace and many prayers, Anna not only survived but thrived. She lived with several health issues, but none serious enough to cause concern until a day just before her thirteenth birthday, when she was admitted to the hospital with an undiagnosed, life-threatening illness. As her condition declined, Anna's parents prayed for God to save her. Then, weary and worried, Crystal gave in to God's will. "Heavenly Father," she prayed, "Thy will be done." The next day, a specialist diagnosed Anna's problem, treatment began, and she lived.

When we're challenged, it can be so hard to submit to God's will. It was even hard for Jesus when He prayed in Gethsemane in Luke 22:42. But He knew that His Father's ways had a deeper purpose than what He wanted. Crystal knew it too. Whatever situation we face, God will bring us through it. Even if we don't get the outcome we want, He will make us spiritually strong.

Lord God, give me strength to submit to You. Thy will be done. Amen.

A MODEL FOR PRAYER

And it came to pass, that, as he was praying in a certain place, when he ceased, one of his disciples said unto him, Lord, teach us to pray.

LUKE 11:1 KJV

Imagine praying like Jesus. When His disciples saw Jesus praying, they said, "Lord, teach us to pray." In Matthew 6:9–13, Jesus responded by giving them the following prayer:

> *Our Father which art in heaven, Hallowed be thy name. Thy kingdom come. Thy will be done in earth, as it is in heaven. Give us this day our daily bread. And forgive us our debts, as we forgive our debtors. And lead us not into temptation, but deliver us from evil: For thine is the kingdom, and the power, and the glory, for ever. Amen.*

With these words, Jesus gave us a four-part model for prayer:

1. **Give** praise to God.
2. **Submit** to His will.
3. **Ask** for your needs to be met, for forgiveness of your sins, and to be protected from evil.
4. **Surrender** it all to God to work out through His power and for His glory.

When you learn to pray like this, then you will be praying like Jesus.

Lord, teach me to pray. Amen.

CHAZAH!

O Lord, how many are Your works! You made them all in wisdom. The earth is full of what You have made.

PSALM 104:24 NLV

Do you love to travel? Perhaps you have visited magnificent mountains, hills, valleys, and deserts. Maybe you have sailed the oceans to faraway lands and, along the way, met some beautiful people and sampled some wonderful coffees. Even if you don't have the means to travel, you can be an "armchair traveler" and see the world's beauty through books, photos, and videos.

In Hebrew, the word *chazah* means "to behold; to gaze at and contemplate with pleasure." Wherever you are right now, there is beauty to behold. Gaze out the window and behold God's works. Contemplate with pleasure what you see. Each day brings something new. The colors of the sunrise, shape-shifting clouds, buds forming on trees... Enjoy it. Take your coffee time with Jesus outdoors. Pour your favorite brew into a travel mug and go for a walk or drive. Behold the works of the Lord and the beauty of the earth. The world is full of what He has made. Look around you. Soak it all in. Chazah! It's a beautiful, wonderful day!

Oh, Lord, thank You for Your beautiful creations. They bring me pleasure every day. Amen.

ASHAMED

Why do You hide Your face, and think of me as one who hates You?

JOB 13:24 NLV

Donna's niece often confided in her. Sometimes, Donna wished she didn't know some of what her niece told her, but she respected her wish to keep things confidential.

"God will punish me for the rest of my life for all the bad stuff I've done," said her niece. "I don't pray anymore because God must hate me."

"If you ask God to forgive you, He will," Donna told her. "You don't have to beg or do anything else to make up for what you've done. God doesn't hate you. Whatever you've done, God will never hate you. He loves you all the time. Just try harder to do better."

It comforted her niece knowing she didn't have to hide from God. He already knew she was ashamed, but He still loved her. He would give her a fresh start.

Maybe you know someone like Donna's niece whose shame makes them hide from God. Do your best to let them know that God loves and forgives them. Encourage them to accept His forgiveness and live in His love.

Dear Jesus, I am a sinner and ashamed of my sin. Forgive me and wash my sins away. Amen.

JESUS ALWAYS, JESUS FOREVER

But Ruth said, "Do not beg me to leave you or turn away from following you. I will go where you go. I will live where you live. Your people will be my people. And your God will be my God. I will die where you die, and there I will be buried."

RUTH 1:16–17 NLV

The book of Ruth holds the beautiful story of a loving friendship between Ruth and her mother-in-law, Naomi. After both women were widowed, Naomi told Ruth to return to her family. But Ruth refused and promised to stay with Naomi. It was a selfless act of devotion and love.

When you married your husband, you pledged your selfless love to him, and there are likely others—family members and friends—whom you will love and care for until the day you die. As wonderful as these earthy relationships are, there is one even better: our relationship with Jesus. His love for us is perfect and complete. Jesus gave His life so we can live with Him forever in heaven. Jesus always. Jesus forever. Nothing, not even death, can separate us from His love.

Jesus, my Savior, wherever I go, You will go. Nothing will separate me from Your never-ending loyalty and devotion—and I am so grateful. Amen.

NOT AS IT SEEMS

"Stop judging by mere appearances,
but instead judge correctly."
JOHN 7:24 NIV

Just before dawn on a cold February morning, residents in Wisconsin saw an array of ghostly white orbs in the sky. Hundreds circled over the Lake Michigan shore. People captured the images on their phones and sent them to the local television stations. What were they? Some thought an adversary was spying on them. Others thought aliens. No. They were seagulls! The atmosphere that morning was just right for light to reflect off their feathers, making the birds look like mysterious objects in the sky.

The Bible tells us to be wise about what we see, because some things are not as they seem. This is true not only when we can't identify what we see but also when we perceive what a person is like by how she or he looks. First Samuel 16:7 says not to judge by appearance but by what is in a person's heart. Wisdom means making a careful and critical examination and finding the facts before we pass judgment on someone (or something). As Christians, it is our duty to judge correctly, to view the world through God's eyes and do what is right.

Lord, if I must judge, then lead me to
judge fairly and correctly. Amen.

LIVE TO PLEASE HIM

It is not the most important thing to me what you or any other people think of me. Even what I think of myself does not mean much.

1 CORINTHIANS 4:3 NLV

Paul is the author of today's scripture verse. He was writing about the criticism he and others faced as they shared the gospel. The story of Jesus' resurrection seemed so unbelievable that some people thought the disciples were crazy. In 1 Corinthians 4:13, Paul wrote: "People think of us as dirt that is worth nothing and as the worst thing on earth to this day." The men and women who shared the gospel were often misunderstood. Still, they continued to preach it, never ashamed to be Jesus' disciples or afraid to be shunned for their faithfulness to Him. The most important thing to Paul was what Jesus thought of him, not what others thought, or even what he thought of himself.

If people criticize us for our faith, we can remember what Paul said and not let the criticism get to us. As long as we live to please Jesus, it's not important what others think.

Dear Jesus, what matters most is what You think of me. Guide me to live in ways that please You. Amen.

JUST JESUS

I made up my mind that while I was with you I would speak of nothing except Jesus Christ and of His death on the cross.

1 CORINTHIANS 2:2 NLV

How do you like your coffee? Do you add cream or sugar? Flavored syrups and sauces and other add-ins are popular, especially at coffee shops. Or maybe you prefer your coffee black. Die-hard black-coffee drinkers opt for the smooth taste of strong black coffee. They believe nothing added is the best way to savor the taste of the roasted beans—just coffee is all they need.

If coffee had existed in New Testament times, we can assume that Paul would have preferred it black. He was a no-nonsense guy, a man firm in what He believed. Paul thought of Jesus day and night. He preached the gospel without ceasing. He preached it clearly—nothing added—just the pure irrefutable gospel. He wrote to the church in Corinth, "I made up my mind that while I was with you I would speak of nothing except Jesus Christ and of His death on the cross." For Paul, there was nothing better than Jesus. Nothing else. Just Him.

Jesus is all we need too.

Lord Jesus, if I have You, I have all I need. You alone are enough. Amen.

IN THE DARKNESS

Your Word is a lamp to my feet and a light to my path.
PSALM 119:105 NLV

The power went out in the storm, and now Marsha sat alone in the darkness at her kitchen table. The house felt empty with her husband on a business trip and their children away at college. Several lit candles provided just enough light to read by, so Marsha reached for the Bible she had left on the table that morning. She turned to the book of Psalms and randomly read through them. She thought of David when he wrote them and how he found strength, solace, and peace with the Lord, even on the darkest nights. David's words brought Marsha comfort. She felt less alone. The Spirit of God was with her.

Whether it's a power outage or something else, whatever kind of darkness you face, God's Word will give you light. Keep a Bible nearby so it's there whenever you need it. It will be your companion when you feel lonely, your comfort when you are sad, and your peace when you feel anxious or afraid. The presence of God will be with you as you read. He will light a path so you can find your way through the darkness.

Lord, You are my light. Your Word brings me comfort and peace. Amen.

WE WILL LEAD YOU

He leadeth me in the paths of righteousness for his name's sake.

Psalm 23:3 KJV

Darcy grew up near forests and woodlands. As a child, she loved hiking with her dad as he taught her nature's secrets and how to mark trails. College and a career moved Darcy to a big city where she lived now with her husband and two girls. One day during a phone call, she said, "Dad, the girls are old enough now. When we visit this summer, will you take them hiking? I want you to show them everything you taught me."

"We'll show them together," her father said.

Together, Darcy and her dad led the girls through the woods, teaching them to mark their path so they wouldn't get lost. One generation leading another, and another, in the right way to go.

As parents, it is our job to lead our children down the right path and to teach them to mark a trail of righteousness so they won't get lost in life. When we pass down what we've learned, we can hope they will pass it from their generation to the next and the next.

Jesus, help me to teach my children what I have learned from You. Lord, lead them and guide them down the right path. Amen.

A PLACE AT THE TABLE

"For where two or three are gathered together in My name, there I am with them."
MATTHEW 18:20 NLV

The women's outreach committee met monthly to brainstorm ideas for maximizing their church's ministry. When they gathered at Laura's house for lunch, the women noticed an extra place set at her table. "Who else is coming?" one asked. "I've set that place for Jesus," Laura said, "to remind us that He's with us." It became their tradition. From that day forward, whenever the women met for lunch, Jesus had a place at their table.

Jesus wants a place at our tables too. Wherever we go, He wants to sit with us, talk with us, and be an integral part of our thoughts and decision-making. Jesus doesn't only deserve a place at our table, He should sit at the head of it. Imagine living in Jesus' time, inviting Him to your home, and then not offering Him the seat of honor. Whether literally or figuratively, set a place for Jesus at your table. When you sit there with family or friends, include Him in your discussions. When you welcome Jesus at your table, He will make a place for you at His.

Come, Lord Jesus, sit with us at our table and be our honored guest. Amen.

GOD AT THE CENTER

God is in the center of her. She will not be moved. God will help her when the morning comes.

Psalm 46:5 NLV

Psalm 46:1–3 says, "God is our safe place and our strength. He is always our help when we are in trouble. So we will not be afraid, even if the earth is shaken and the mountains fall into the center of the sea, and even if its waters go wild with storm and the mountains shake with its action." The psalm speaks of a city with God at its center. Whatever comes to destroy that city, it will not fail. Like today's verse reminds us, "God will help her when the morning comes."

We are that city. Trouble may come. We will go through tough times, but through it all, God will be with us. By putting our faith and trust in Him, we will not fall. We will not fail. Our all-powerful and loving God is the one who guides us through our troubles and helps us rebuild. He is our strong place and our safe place. With God at the center of our lives, we will stand and keep standing.

Lord God, I will put my faith and trust in You, my safe place and my ever-present help in times of trouble. Amen.

I SHALL NOT BE MOVED

Good will come to the man. . .whose hope is in the Lord. He will be like a tree planted by the water, that sends out its roots by the river. It will not be afraid when the heat comes. . .in a dry year, or stop giving fruit.

JEREMIAH 17:7–8 NLV

Imagine a tree, centuries old, planted near a river. Countless dry spells and storms couldn't bring it down. The lyrics of this African American spiritual were inspired by the tree in today's scripture:

I shall not be, I shall not be moved.
I shall not be, I shall not be moved;
Like a tree planted by the water,
I shall not be moved.
When my cross is heavy, I shall not be moved,
When my cross is heavy, I shall not be moved;
Like a tree planted by the water,
I shall not be moved.

This is one of many encouraging songs and hymns. You know some of them. Sing them when you feel worried or afraid. Let their melodies and words lift you to the high place where our heavenly Father lives. He will be your strength. Like that tree planted near the water, you shall not be moved.

Lord, I lift my voice to You in song. Whatever trouble I face, I will not be moved. Amen.

HE LIFTS ME UP

She is clothed with strength and dignity;
she can laugh at the days to come.

PROVERBS 31:25 NIV

He was ten years older than her when he convinced her to run away to get married. She was just eighteen. The first weeks of their marriage were heaven, but then things changed. He drank heavily and became abusive. Still, she stayed with him. Then, almost fifteen years into their marriage, he shot and killed a man and was sentenced to life in prison without parole. Her family and friends had criticized her all along for staying with him. She knew they were right, but they didn't understand that fear and insecurity had made her stay. She had turned to the Lord for strength, and now, finally free from her husband's abuse, she stood tall with dignity. God had led her out of danger and into a new and better life.

Youthful mistakes, bad company, getting caught up in the sins of others. . .whatever brings us down, God can lift us up. He brings us through our troubles, washes away our sins, and helps us face criticism of our past with dignity and strength. He is the God of fresh starts and better days.

Restore my strength and dignity, Lord.
Give me a fresh, new life. Amen.

HE MAKES ME STRONG

"Many women do noble things, but you surpass them all."
PROVERBS 31:29 NIV

The song "I Am Woman," written by Helen Reddy, topped the charts in the early 1970s. Reddy said that some of her inspiration for the song was the strong women in her own family, women who had weathered the storms of the Great Depression, world wars, and abusive relationships. The lyrics celebrate that strong women are invincible. They can't be defeated. For decades women have been encouraged by that message.

When you read your Bible, you will discover women who refused to be defeated but drew their strength from the Lord, including Deborah, Esther, Jochebed, Mary, and others. They faced their troubles, didn't back down, and emerged defiant and strong. These women, along with strong women you know today, are examples of God's power working through them.

Many women accomplish noble things, but those relying on the Lord's strength surpass them. They call on Him for help, and then with Him leading the way, they go into battle with victory as their goal. When women get their power from Him, all things are possible.

Whatever you need today, you can count on Jesus to supply it. Keep going. Stay strong!

Lord God, because of You I will not be defeated. I am invincible. Amen.

MOTHER KNOWS BEST

She opens her mouth with wisdom.
The teaching of kindness is on her tongue.

PROVERBS 31:26 NLV

"Mom, you were right. I should have been brave and asked her." Dana's son had wanted to ask a certain girl to the dance, but assuming she wouldn't go out with him, he had asked someone else. Afterward, he learned from a friend that the girl he'd wanted to ask would have said yes. "I messed up," he said.

"So, what do you plan to do?" Dana asked him.

"I'm going to find a way to go with her."

Dana had taught her son to be wise about his decisions, but like most teens, he didn't always listen. "Wouldn't that be unkind?" she said. "It would really hurt the girl you asked. Take her to the dance and have fun. Who knows, maybe you'll find out that you want to go out with her again."

She could have lectured her son about his decision, but instead, with gentle words, she taught him the best way to handle the situation. Advising our teens can be challenging, but when we offer our wisdom with kindness, kids are more likely to respond.

Jesus, give me patience. Help me to be calm and think about my words when teaching my children right from wrong. Amen.

MOTHERHOOD IS THE HARDEST JOB

Whatever work you do, do it with all your heart.
Do it for the Lord. . . . You will get your reward. . . .
He will give you what you should receive.

COLOSSIANS 3:23–24 NLV

God gave mothers the hardest job of all: raising babies from birth to adulthood. Moms can expect at least eighteen years of caregiving, leading, encouraging, reprimanding, and teaching until their babies leave the nest. It's not a job for the faint of heart. Still, mothers give it their best.

Motherhood can be a thankless job too. Moms are always busy looking out for everyone in their household. Along with their day jobs, mothers cook, clean, do laundry, shop for groceries, and act as chauffeurs to afterschool activities. Then, at night, they fall into bed to recharge for the next day.

So much of what moms do is taken for granted—but take heart, because God knows. He says to mothers, "Good job!" When they raise their children to honor Him, God promises them a reward. And what better reward than receiving God-loving adult children who will honor and care for their mothers for the rest of their lives?

Jesus, I will do my best to raise children who honor and respect both You and me. Lord, lead me to lead them. Amen.

BETTER "LATTE" THAN NEVER

Return to the Lord your God, for He is full of loving-kindness and loving-pity. He is slow to anger, full of love, and ready to keep His punishment from you.

JOEL **2:13** NLV

"I've been praying for you," Sonja told her friend Carolyn. "I'm so sorry you lost your job. The timing couldn't be worse."

Carolyn lifted her coffee cup as if making a toast. "Thanks for the prayers," she answered with a hint of sarcasm. "I haven't prayed in years."

"Why not?" Sonja asked.

"I was raised to be religious," said Carolyn, "but when I grew up, I stopped going to church and I stopped praying."

"I've seen prayer work," Sonja said, and then she shared some examples with Carolyn.

"Well then keep on praying for me, I guess."

"And you pray too!" Sonja told her. "Better late than never." As she drank her latte, Sonja prayed silently that Carolyn would return to the Lord. She wanted her friend to experience His loving-kindness.

If you haven't prayed for a while, come back to Jesus. He is waiting for you. He will forgive you for not speaking with Him. Jesus loves you and is ready to help with all of your needs.

Dear Jesus, it's been a long time, but I'm here now to pray. Amen.

THE SCAM

A wise man sees sin and hides himself,
but the foolish go on, and are punished for it.
PROVERBS 22:3 NLV

A woman and a man had been communicating through a dating app for Christian seniors. After chatting for a while, they met for coffee. The man told her that he had been a financial planner. He turned their conversation to finances, and during that one coffee date he acquired enough information from her to hack into one of her credit cards and make purchases. Then he disappeared. He had given her a false name, and they had only communicated through the app. *It was foolish of me,* she told herself. *I should have known better.* She had felt something urging her not to give him so much information, but she had been taken in by his charm.

There are many scams today, and we need wisdom not to fall for them. The Holy Spirit had been trying to tell the woman to stop discussing her finances with the man, but she didn't listen. She had learned, though, not to be fooled again.

When meeting someone new, we should be wise with our trust. While there are many good people in the world, some are demons in disguise.

Lord, give me wisdom about whom I should trust. Amen.

THE HOLY SPIRIT

"Would any of you fathers give your son a stone if he asked for bread? Or would you give a snake if he asked for a fish?. . . You are sinful and you know how to give good things to your children. How much more will your Father in heaven give the Holy Spirit to those who ask Him?"

LUKE 11:11, 13 NLV

God knows what His children need. One of His greatest gifts to us is the Holy Spirit. The Holy Spirit guides, comforts, strengthens, and prays for us. He is the one who speaks to our hearts and urges us to do what is right. He makes us aware of sin so we won't get caught in Satan's traps. In troubled times, the Holy Spirit provides us with peace beyond our understanding. And when we don't know how to pray, the Holy Spirit intercedes for us.

When we pray, we should remember to ask God to fill our hearts with the Holy Spirit and guide us to feel His urgings and hear His words. Through the Holy Spirit, we learn to walk with Jesus, do His work, and become more like Him.

Lord God, pour Your Holy Spirit into my heart and give me keen awareness of His presence within me. Amen.

"LOVE YOU!"

My children, let us not love with words or in talk only. Let us love by what we do and in truth.

1 John 3:18 NLV

"Love you." The words trip off the tongue, easy to say as if they were a ritual. Parents send their kids off to school. "Love you." Wives kiss their husbands goodbye as they leave for work. "Love you." Teen girls say it to each other all the time. "Love you!" As nice as the words are to hear, what do they mean?

Today's verse reminds us that love is so much more than words. We show love through actions. Love is more than hugs and kisses. It is faithfulness in our commitment to care for one another. It is putting the needs of others before our own, helping the hungry and the poor, and giving of our time, attention, and resources. Love is forgiveness and understanding. It is teaching our children right from wrong and leading them to Jesus. Love isn't always easy. It is caring for the sick, praying for the lost, holding a hand, and wiping away a tear. Love is Jesus in us working through us.

"Love you." Think about those words. What more can you do to show your love?

Jesus, teach me to love through my actions and in truth. Amen.

WHAT IS LOVE?

If I have the gift of speaking God's Word and if I understand all secrets, but do not have love, I am nothing. If I know all things and if I have the gift of faith so I can move mountains, but do not have love, I am nothing.

1 Corinthians 13:2 NLV

Some scripture is so familiar we don't stop to think about its deeper meaning. For example, Paul's definition of love in 1 Corinthians 13:4–8: "Love does not give up. Love is kind. Love is not jealous. Love does not put itself up as being important. Love has no pride. Love does not do the wrong thing. Love never thinks of itself. Love does not get angry. Love does not remember the suffering that comes from being hurt by someone. Love is not happy with sin. Love is happy with the truth. Love takes everything that comes without giving up. Love believes all things. Love hopes for all things. Love keeps on in all things. Love never comes to an end."

As you have coffee with Jesus this morning, stop and think about Paul's words. Ask yourself how they apply to your relationships with others.

Dear Jesus, instill in me a deeper meaning of love, and help me to love others as You love me. Amen.

THE WARRIOR HUSBAND

Better a patient person than a warrior,
one with self-control than one who takes a city.
Proverbs 16:32 NIV

Sherry's husband thought of himself as a warrior. His self-confidence was so strong, he believed there was nothing he couldn't do. If something around the house needed to get done, he hurried to do it. The problem was that his skill set didn't always match the task—but he wouldn't admit it. This meant long hours redoing what he had done and multiple trips to the hardware store. Sherry loved her warrior husband. She had learned patience from living with and loving him. She wished, though, that he had more patience. She often prayed, "Lord, before he starts a project, please make him stop and think."

First Corinthians 13:4 says that "love is patient." Isn't it ironic that we can learn patience from impatient people like Sherry's husband? The same is true of other elements of love. We can learn forgiveness from those who are unforgiving, humility from those who have pride, and selflessness from those who are selfish. The Lord has a way of teaching us to love through the actions of others.

Lord, teach me to be patient with those who are impatient and prideful. Help me to treat them with love. Amen.

LOVE DOESN'T GIVE UP

We know that troubles help us learn not to give up.

Romans 5:3 NLV

Audrey's son had rejected every loving thing she had done to help him overcome addiction. She didn't give up. She loved him through Jesus by praying for him persistently. She told him, "I'm not giving up on you." How beautiful it is when actions back up those words.

1 Corinthians 13:7 reminds us, "Love takes everything that comes without giving up. Love believes all things. Love hopes for all things. Love keeps on in all things." Love means not giving up on others when they go through troubles. Love means supporting a family member with cancer, consoling a friend who's heartsick over a loss, and helping a child reach a goal. Love means encouragement. Love means prayer. Loving someone through their troubles can be hard. It can hurt. But godly love is learning how not to give up. Love goes hand in hand with hope. When we love like Jesus and put our hope in Him, then—in all things—love keeps on and love will prevail.

Lord Jesus, love is the antidote for all kinds of trouble. Teach me to love without giving up. Amen.

BE AN EXAMPLE

Those who do not love do not know God because God is love.

1 John 4:8 NLV

The love we experience on earth is connected to our humanity. Only in heaven will we truly understand the complexity and depth of God's love. While we are still here, though, we can know enough about His love to share it with others in ways that reflect how He loves us.

Those who don't know God don't understand the kind of love that remains calm in anger, is patient with those who are impatient, and forgives those who don't deserve it.

Each day when studying your Bible, praying, and reading devotions, you grow nearer to God. As you learn more about Him and His immeasurable goodness, you also grow in your capacity to love. The time spent with the Lord has taught you to love the way He loves you: patiently, persistently, and with forgiveness. One way you can lead others to know God is to be an example of His love, to love through kindness, service, to love unselfishly, and to love in situations where love usually doesn't exist. First Corinthians 16:14 says it best: "Everything you do should be done in love."

Lord God, please guide others to know You through the love I show them. Amen.

TURNING 100

My body and my heart may grow weak, but God is the strength of my heart and all I need forever.

PSALM 73:26 NLV

A reporter for a local newspaper was assigned to interview honorees at a luncheon for seniors turning one hundred years old. She asked each person about their secret to longevity. "Do a crossword puzzle every day," said one. "Get a dog or cat," said another. They spoke of what they ate or drank, how much they exercised, and time spent with family and friends. Some of the answers were humorous. When one caused raucous laughter, a woman shouted, "I wish I had heard that." The last person interviewed was a quiet gentleman sitting by himself. When the reporter asked him about his secret to living a long life, his answer was simple: "God."

If the Lord blesses us with a hundred years and a luncheon in our honor, we can praise Him for a good, long life. But we aren't promised a long life. Our bodies will eventually become old and weak; however, if our hearts remain strong and filled with love for God, then we have the promise of eternal life in heaven.

Dear Lord, when my life here on earth is complete and You call me home, I look forward to spending eternity with You. Amen.

OUR CALLING

I have fought a good fight. I have finished the work I was to do. I have kept the faith.

2 Timothy 4:7 NLV

As Paul neared the end of his life, he encouraged his friends to continue his work here on earth. In 2 Timothy 4:2–5, he said, "Use the Word of God to show people they are wrong. Use the Word of God to help them do right. You must be willing to wait for people to understand what you teach as you teach them. The time will come when people will not listen to the truth. They will look for teachers who will tell them only what they want to hear. They will not listen to the truth. Instead, they will listen to stories made up by men. You must watch for all these things."

Paul's calling was to lead others to Jesus. He had worked selflessly and faithfully. Teaching the gospel was the greatest accomplishment of his life. Like Paul, our greatest accomplishment should be doing the work Jesus called us to do: sharing the gospel. Tell someone about Jesus today. Help them understand the true meaning of God's Word.

Jesus, I will never be shy about sharing the gospel. Lead me to those who need to hear it. Amen.

NO WORRIES

Worry in the heart of a man weighs it down,
but a good word makes it glad.
PROVERBS 12:25 NLV

The church custodian, Pete, was a quiet older man. He made sure his work didn't disturb the pastor's meetings or the worship team's rehearsals. He saved noisy jobs for evenings when no one was around. If asked to do something, Pete always smiled and said, "No worries." He got right to work. When called on a cold Saturday night for a furnace problem, Pete said, "No worries." He labored through the night so the church would be warm for the Sunday service. People referred to him as "No Worries Pete." They knew they could trust him to get the job done.

Pete had learned to give his worries to Jesus and trust Him to work things out. Jesus had never let Pete down. Pete became an example of the Lord by using his skills to ease the worries of others. When there was something that needed cleaning or fixing, his cheerful, "No worries" was just what church leaders needed to calm their anxious hearts.

Whatever is on your mind today, tell yourself, "No worries. Jesus can handle it." You can trust Him. He will never let you down.

Lord, thank You for reminding me not to worry.
You have everything under control. Amen.

WORRY LESS, PRAY MORE

Do not worry. Learn to pray about everything. Give thanks to God as you ask Him for what you need. The peace of God is much greater than the human mind can understand. This peace will keep your hearts and minds through Christ Jesus.

PHILIPPIANS 4:6–7 NLV

"As if I don't have enough to worry about, the dog's been throwing up and I have to get him to the vet." Kristen sighed. "So what else is bothering you?" her sister asked. "My job, the kids' grades, what to make for dinner, and world peace," Kristen answered. "I don't know. I'm just stressed out."

Life can turn stressful when things seem to pile one atop the other. That's why it's wise to pray as those worries come along and ask Jesus to take them. If we shift our thoughts to thanking Him for His blessings, we will begin to calm down. Those working in time management sometimes offer this quote: "The shorter way to do many things is to only do one thing at a time." If we give our worries to Jesus one at a time and allow Him to help us, we might find out we worry less and accomplish more.

Dear Jesus, You know what I'm worried about. Let's work it out together. Amen.

A CUP OF JOE

"You planned to do a bad thing to me. But God planned it for good. . . . So do not be afraid. I will take care of you and your little ones." He gave them comfort and words of kindness.

GENESIS 50:20–21 NLV

One of the most powerful lessons about forgiveness is found in the story of Joseph. When Joseph was a teen, his brothers sold him into slavery. Many years later, Joseph had become a man of power in Egypt. Because of his wisdom, the people of Egypt and its surrounding areas, including Joseph's family, were saved from starvation during a long famine. Joseph was reunited with his brothers, and they worried he would seek revenge for what they had done to him. Instead, Joseph said that his years of suffering had been a blessing. Had things not happened as they did, the people might not have been saved. He forgave his brothers, and he did it with words of comfort and kindness.

As you relax savoring a steaming cup of joe, read Joseph's story in Genesis 37–50. See what else you can learn from this great man.

Lord God, You plan it all for good, even when things go wrong. Please help me to be like Joseph and forgive those who hurt me. Amen.

LESSONS FROM THE CROSS

Then Jesus said, "Father, forgive them. They do not know what they are doing."
LUKE 23:34 NLV

Jesus hung there nailed to the cross—battered, bleeding, and in excruciating pain. He had done nothing wrong to deserve all they had done to Him, and yet, knowing God would judge them, He prayed. He asked God to forgive them. Had they known the one true God, listened to His words and followed them, they would have believed Jesus was the Messiah. But they didn't. They had no idea what they were doing. Instead of worshipping Him, they tortured and killed Him.

As Jesus was dying for the forgiveness of our sins, His words provided yet another lesson, an example of how we should forgive those who hurt us. When people cause us suffering and pain, we can pray His prayer, "Father, forgive them. They do not know what they are doing." Those words lift from our shoulders the burden of judgment and releases it to God. Asking God to forgive those who hurt us is also a lesson about mercy. Until His last breath, by His example Jesus was still teaching us from the cross.

Lord God, please forgive those who hurt me. Be merciful to them. Lead them to know You as the one true God. Amen.

THE OTHER JOSEPH

Trust in the Lord with all your heart, and do not trust in your own understanding. Agree with Him in all your ways, and He will make your paths straight.

PROVERBS 3:5–6 NLV

Now, let's see what we can learn from another Joseph, Mary's husband in the New Testament.

While Joseph was engaged to Mary, she became pregnant with Jesus, even though she was a virgin. When Joseph found out, he planned to call off the marriage, thinking that she had been with another man. But in Matthew 1:20–21, an angel from the Lord came to Joseph in a dream. "Do not be afraid to take Mary as your wife. She is to become a mother by the Holy Spirit. A Son will be born to her. You will give Him the name Jesus because He will save His people from the punishment of their sins."

Joseph trusted what the angel told him. Had he not, think about how the story of Jesus' birth might have changed. Joseph is a great example of trusting God when we can't understand where He is leading us and why. Read Joseph's story in Matthew 1:18–25.

Dear Jesus, when I can't understand Your ways, help me to trust You with all my heart. Amen.

WHAT CHILDREN CAN TEACH US

But Jesus said, "Let the little children come to Me. Do not stop them. The holy nation of heaven is made up of ones like these."

MATTHEW 19:14 NLV

"Mom, how can God see everyone at the same time?" asked little Jackson.

"Because he can be everywhere at the same time," his mother answered.

"Like a superhero?"

"Better than a superhero."

"Okay," said Jackson, running off to play.

Little children are very accepting of a simple answer. Unlike adults, they don't spend much time analyzing, fact checking, and evaluating. Their innocence is refreshing. There is much we can learn by observing our little ones, including humility, trust, perseverance, overcoming challenges, dependence, forgiveness, and acceptance. Their lives are pure and simple, free from the clutter of adulthood. Maybe that's what Jesus meant when he said, "The holy nation of heaven is made up of ones like these."

When we get to heaven someday, all the grown-up clutter will be gone and we will be like innocent children again: dependent on God, accepting of what is, humble, forgiving, and trusting. Don't miss out on what young children can teach you. Let them come to you. See what you can learn.

Dear Jesus, open my eyes, ears, and heart to the simple lessons I can learn from a child. Amen.

NEW KID ON THE BLOCK

For if a man belongs to Christ, he is a new person. The old life is gone. New life has begun.

2 CORINTHIANS 5:17 NLV

Lisa had recently asked Jesus into her heart. This very young, unmarried mother had never been to church or read the Bible. She was eager now to learn more about Jesus, so she began attending the church at the end of her block. Lisa didn't understand much of what the pastor preached, so she joined a Bible study class. She asked questions like, "Is everyone in the Bible real?" When she learned something new, Lisa often interjected, "That's so cool!" As her enthusiasm grew, she felt others in the group were annoyed by her questions and quick reactions. Feeling unaccepted, Lisa quit.

New believers can be somewhat like little children, eager to learn about God and surprised by the goodness and wonder they find. It's our duty as more-experienced Christians to accept them where they are and help them grow. How sad that Lisa had no one willing to mentor her. What a lost opportunity to lead her to become a new person with a new and exciting life.

Lord, whenever I can, help me to guide new believers to a loving relationship with You. Amen.

KEEP HOPE ALIVE

I would have been without hope if I had not believed that I would see the loving-kindness of the Lord in the land of the living. Wait for the Lord. Be strong. Let your heart be strong. Yes, wait for the Lord.

Psalm 27:13–14 NLV

Madison and Alan had planned to start their family as soon as they were married, but Madison wasn't able to conceive. They had almost accepted that she would never get pregnant when, after three years, she gave birth to a son. Tragically, he was stillborn. The pain of his loss was lasting, raw, and deep. The couple prayed, asking God not to allow them to get pregnant again if He planned to take their baby. "Thy will be done," they prayed. They remained childless, but not hopeless. Seven years later, Madison awoke feeling sick to her stomach. Nine months after that, she gave birth to a healthy baby girl.

Hoping is hard after a tragic loss like that of Madison and Alan's, but if we keep hope alive and wait for the Lord, miracles are possible. They often come when we least expect them.

Dear Jesus, please hear our persistent prayer. We remain strong in our hope, and we trust in Your goodness. Thy will be done. Amen.

THE DISCIPLE JESUS LOVED

There are many other things which Jesus did also. If they were all written down, I do not think the world itself could hold the books that would be written.

JOHN 21:25 NLV

John is known as the disciple Jesus loved. Of course, Jesus loved all His disciples. But in addition to being one of the twelve chosen by Jesus, John was Jesus' close friend, His best friend. Imagine the complexity of their relationship. They had a deep earthly friendship, and John likely felt about Jesus the way we do our closest friend. Along with that, John knew who Jesus was: the Messiah, the Son of God, God Himself. How overwhelming that must have been for the disciple Jesus loved.

John's gospel reads somewhat like a eulogy. He writes about being present for most of Jesus' miracles. He witnessed his friend's crucifixion and was asked by Jesus, from the cross, to care for His mother, Mary. John was at the empty tomb and at Jesus' transfiguration. John ends his Gospel by saying there is so much more he could tell us about his friend, Lord, and Savior. We can only wonder and imagine!

Dear Jesus, oh, how I wish I knew everything John could tell us about You, all the wonderful and amazing things You did here on earth. Amen.

BEYOND WORDS

I pray that you will be able to understand how wide and how long and how high and how deep His love is.

EPHESIANS 3:18 NLV

Paul hadn't witnessed any of what Jesus did on earth, but he still understood that Jesus had deep love for us. In Ephesians 3:18, Paul prays that we too will understand the depth of His love.

David tried putting it into words in Psalm 36:5–9: "O Lord, Your loving-kindness goes to the heavens. You are as faithful as the sky is high. You are as right and good as mountains are big. You are as fair when You judge as a sea is deep. O Lord, You keep safe both man and animal. Of what great worth is Your loving-kindness, O God! The children of men come and are safe in the shadow of Your wings. They are filled with the riches of Your house. And You give them a drink from Your river of joy. All life came from You. In Your light we see light."

God's love is so deep, it is beyond anything we humans can understand or even put into words. But we know this: He loves us now and will love us forever.

O Lord! Fill up my heart with Your deep, never-ending love. Amen.

GOD IN US

No one has ever seen God; but if we love one another, God lives in us and his love is made complete in us.

1 John 4:12 NIV

No one on earth has seen God the Father as He exists in heaven, but He can be seen through God the Son who has been with God forever and has lived here, among us, on earth. When we read in the Bible about Jesus' many acts of love, His compassion, gentleness, and caring, we see God's love. The better we know Him, the more we can love one another in the ways He loves us.

We experience His love through the acts of others. We feel it in their faithfulness, goodness, kindness, and generosity. We experience God's love in acts of mercy and forgiveness, especially when it isn't deserved. God's love is apparent in gentleness and caring, both toward people and animals (Psalm 36:6). It is felt when we comfort one another and help each other. God is in every act of love because God *is* love!

With God living in us, His Holy Spirit helps us to love others unselfishly, as Jesus loves us. When we imitate the ways Jesus loves us, we share God's love—and in sharing, His love is made complete.

Lord, make Your love complete in me. Amen.

NEVER WILL I EVER

Peter said to Jesus, "Even if all men give up and turn away because of You, I will never."
MATTHEW 26:33 NLV

At the Last Supper, Jesus told His disciples that all of them would be ashamed of Him and leave Him. "Even if everyone turns away from You, I never will," said Peter. "Before a rooster crows tonight, you will deny me three times," said the Lord. Matthew 26:35 tells us that Peter responded, "Even if I have to die with You, I will never say I do not know You."

We can imagine Peter, a leader among the disciples, as self-confident, outspoken, maybe a little arrogant, and very sure of his faith. But after Jesus was arrested, Peter *did* deny Him three times. Maybe this brought Peter down from his self-confident faith and taught him some humility. The Bible says he went outside and cried loud cries, perhaps because His faith had failed. After Jesus' death, Peter was relentless in spreading the gospel. He never again denied Jesus, and in the end, Peter did die for Him, sentenced to death by Nero.

Peter's story is one of second chances. His faith had failed him once, but he learned—and it didn't fail him again.

Dear Jesus, when my faith fails me, show me why, and let me try again. Amen.

HE WILL FIGHT FOR YOU

"The Lord will fight for you.
All you have to do is keep still."

EXODUS 14:14 NLV

Moses had rescued the Israelites from slavery in Egypt. In Exodus 14, as they reached the Red Sea, they saw Pharaoh and his army coming after them. They panicked. "Moses, why didn't you leave us alone?" they shouted. "What have you done to us? It would be better to be slaves than to die here in the desert!" Moses answered, "Stay strong! The Lord will fight for you. All you have to do is keep still." Then the Lord told Moses to put his hand out toward the sea. The water parted and the Israelites walked through it on dry land to the other side. The Lord told Moses to put his hand toward the sea again. The path closed and the entire Egyptian army was swallowed by the sea.

When we are afraid and our faith is all we have to rely on, we can know that the Lord is with us. He loves and cares for us, and He will help us. When we are afraid, we can trust Him to fight for us. All we have to do is stay strong in our faith and keep still.

Dear Jesus, I don't know what to do.
Please fight for me. Amen.

BE STILL AND KNOW

You will hear of wars and lots of talk about wars, but do not be afraid. These things must happen, but it is not the end yet.

MATTHEW 24:6 NLV

Jesus spoke of the end times. He warned we would hear of wars and rumors of wars. But He also told us, "It is not the end yet." In Matthew 6:34 He reminds us, "Do not worry about tomorrow. Tomorrow will have its own worries. The troubles we have in a day are enough for one day."

Today, we hear of wars often. There's lots of talk about potential wars and how they might impact our lives. If all that talk makes us worried and afraid, we can find comfort in the words of Psalm 46:9–10 (NIV): "He makes wars cease to the ends of the earth. He breaks the bow and shatters the spear; he burns the shields with fire. He says, 'Be still, and know that I am God; I will be exalted among the nations, I will be exalted in the earth.'"

The Lord is in control now and forever. We needn't worry over wars. Instead, be still, trust Him, and know that He is God.

Lord, I know You are in control of all the nations. Help me not to worry or be afraid. Amen.

A QUIET SPIRIT

Your beauty should come from. . .the heart. . . .
Your beauty should be a gentle and quiet spirit.
In God's sight this is of great worth and
no amount of money can buy it.
1 Peter 3:4 NLV

Barbara disliked loud music and noisy crowds. She accompanied her husband and their friends to ball games, fairs, and concerts; but secretly, Barbara couldn't wait to get home, curl up in her favorite chair, and read a book. She loved quiet places. She found peace in the woods, the edge of a stream in the early morning, and late nights when the rest of the world was asleep. Barbara had been born with a quiet and gentle spirit. As much as her husband enjoyed being with people, he admired his wife's quiet soul. He found it attractive.

There is great beauty in a woman with a quiet spirit. She draws people in like a safe port in a storm. Her quiet spirit listens, learns, and is wise. She imparts wisdom gently. Peace flows steadily from her heart and envelops those around her. Her beauty comes not from jewelry, the clothes she wears, or makeup. It comes from deep inside her soul. It is a gift from God, a great and priceless treasure.

. . . .

Lord God, bless me with a quiet spirit. Amen.

PETS IN HEAVEN

For the same thing is to happen to both the sons of men and animals. As one dies, so dies the other. . . . Who knows that the spirit of man goes up and the spirit of the animal goes down to the earth?

ECCLESIASTES 3:19, 21 NLV

Pets are members of our family. When they die, we grieve their loss and wonder if we will see them in heaven. The Bible doesn't tell us if our pets will be in heaven, but we know animals are there. In the book of Revelation, Jesus and his army return to earth on white horses (Revelation 19:11, 14). Isaiah 11:6 prophesied a new earth where animals live in peace with each other: "The wolf will live with the lamb. The leopard will lie down with the baby goat. The calf and the young lion and the young fat animal will lie down together."

Billy Graham thought our pets would be in heaven. He said, "God will prepare everything for our perfect happiness in heaven, and if it takes my dog being there, I believe he'll be there."[8]

We don't know for sure, but we have hope we will see our little friends again.

Dear Jesus, I hope my pets are in heaven. If they are with You, please care for them. Amen.

[8] Elena Tafone, Tess Clarkson, and Rick Hamlin, "The Big Question: Do Animals Go to Heaven?," *Guideposts*, July 22, 2024, https://guideposts.org/angels-and-miracles/miracles/gods-grace/the-big-question-do-animals-go-to-heaven/.

BEHOLD THE BEHEMOTH!

"And these are but the outer fringe of his works; how faint the whisper we hear of him! Who then can understand the thunder of his power?"

JOB 26:14 NIV

The Lord spoke to Job:

> *"Look at Behemoth, which I made along with you and which feeds on grass like an ox. What strength it has in its loins, what power in the muscles of its belly! Its tail sways like a cedar; the sinews of its thighs are close-knit. Its bones are tubes of bronze, its limbs like rods of iron. It ranks first among the works of God, yet its Maker can approach it with his sword." (Job 40:15–19)*

Imagine encountering this huge creature. Would you fight it, or would you run for your life? Some problems we face are like the Behemoth—bigger than we can handle. We can run from them, or we can call on our Maker's power to help and protect us. In the book of Job, God tells Job about His works and His power. But what He said is only a whisper of what He can do. Whatever Behemoth you face in life, God has power over it. Don't run. Stand strong and ask Him to help you.

Lord, with Your mighty power defeat this Behemoth that stands in my way. Amen.

LITTLE THINGS

"Are not two sparrows sold for a penny? Yet not one of them will fall to the ground outside your Father's care."
MATTHEW 10:29 NIV

Civilla Durfee Martin, poet and author of the hymn "His Eye Is on the Sparrow," wrote about what inspired her song: "It was written at the bedside of a bedridden saint. . . . During our conversation I asked her if she did not sometimes get discouraged. She answered, 'How can I be discouraged, when my Father watches the sparrows, and I know He loves and cares for me?' Procuring paper and pencil, in a few moments I wrote the now-famous hymn."[9]

Why should I feel discouraged?
Why should the shadows come?
Why should my heart be lonely
And long for heaven and home,
When Jesus is my portion?
My constant Friend is He:
His eye is on the sparrow,
And I know He watches me.

The little things we see and hear can inspire us. What little thing have you seen today that brought you inspiration or encouragement?

Jesus, open my eyes to see You in the little things all around me. Amen.

[9] Charles H. Gabriel, *The Singers and Their Songs* (Rodeheaver, 1916), 52–53, Archive.org.

STONES OF REMEMBRANCE

"Let this be something special among you. Your children will ask you later, 'What do these stones mean to you?'"

JOSHUA 4:6 NLV

After God helped the Israelites cross the Jordan River into the Promised Land, He told them to make a memorial using twelve stones from the middle of the Jordan to signify the twelve tribes of Israel. The stones would be a lasting remembrance of God's care and guidance. Joshua said to the people, "Let this be something special among you. Your children will ask you later, 'What do these stones mean to you?'" Surely, children did ask and were told of their families' history.

What "stones" can you share with your children? What objects can you show them to tell some of your family's history? The graves of your ancestors are filled with stories. Visit the graves with your children and tell them about the people. Old letters, heirloom jewelry, and notes inside Bibles all have stories to tell. Share the stones of the past with your kids. Remember to share how the Lord has led you. As Joshua said, "Let this be something special among you."

Dear Jesus, remind me of special family members and friends who have died. Guide my words as I tell my children about them and You. Amen.

YOUR TESTIMONY

Oh, thank GOD—he's so good! His love never runs out. All of you set free by GOD, tell the world! Tell how he freed you from oppression.

PSALM 107:2–3 MSG

At meetings of those recovering from an addiction, people often share their recovery stories as a testimony of hope. They speak of who they were and their journey of overcoming their addiction and becoming who they are now. They share what they've learned and the emotional and spiritual growth they've experienced.

As Christians, we also have a testimony. We can tell of where God found us, how He led us, the people who helped us, and what we've learned. Our testimonies are powerful tools, and we should use them as a way of giving others hope and leading them to Christ. We can tailor our stories to the needs of others through similar elements in the stories we share. We needn't sugarcoat details or embellish or emphasize them. When we tell others about our relationship with Jesus, we should allow Him to lead us.

Never shy away from telling your testimony. It could rob others of the opportunity to be set free from sin.

Jesus, thank You for saving me. Help me to tell my story, and may it lead others to You to be saved. Amen.

PAINTED ROCKS

And they will show that the Lord is faithful. He is my rock. There is nothing in Him that is not right and good.

PSALM 92:15 NLV

"Mom, some people are painting small rocks and hiding them for others to find. It's supposed to be a little act of kindness. Can we paint some?"

"Sure," said her mother. "But I have an idea. Let's put a scripture reference on each one and leave it someplace that shows its meaning. Maybe it will lead the finder to the Bible to see what the scripture says."

Mother and daughter painted their rocks. They placed Matthew 6:26 (NCV) near a bird feeder: "Look at the birds in the air. They don't plant or harvest or store food in barns, but your heavenly Father feeds them." They put Psalm 23:2 on the grass at the edge of a stream and Psalm 96:1 at an outdoor concert. With each rock they left, they prayed for God to guide the finder to the verse in the Bible.

If you are looking for a project to do with your kids or grandkids, try painting some scripture rocks. It's a great way to bond with each other while serving the Lord.

Lord, You are my rock. Wherever I go, lead me to share Your Word. Amen.

THE BREAK ROOM

The words of a gossip are like tasty bits of food; people like to gobble them up.
PROVERBS 26:22 NCV

Ashley and Jennifer sat alone in the break room at work drinking coffee. "So, what do you think about Patty and Ramon?" said Ashley.

"What about them?" asked Jennifer.

"You haven't heard? They're having an affair."

Ashley went on to tell Jennifer that her boss, Patty, was seen one night at a bar with their coworker Ramon. Both were married.

The American journalist and gossip columnist Earl Wilson once said, "Science may never come up with a better office communication system than the coffee break."[10] It's true that a plethora of gossip is spread over a cup of coffee. King Solomon observed that gossip is like tasty bits of food that people like to gobble up.

In Leviticus 19:16, the Lord tells us not to spread gossip, and James 1:26 (NLV) reminds us, "If a person thinks he is religious, but does not keep his tongue from speaking bad things, he is fooling himself. His religion is worth nothing." Clearly, God doesn't like gossip in the break room—or anywhere else.

Lord Jesus, help me to tame my tongue and not participate in gossipy conversations. I want the words I say to honor and please You. Amen.

[10] Kelly Kuehn, *"29 Funny Coffee Quotes That Keep the Laughs Brewing," Reader's Digest*, December 12, 2024, https://www.rd.com/article/funny-coffee-quotes/.

DIOTREPHES AND GAIUS

So if I come, I will show what he is doing by the bad things he is saying about us.

3 John 10 NLV

In 3 John 1, John writes to his friend Gaius, praising him for following the truth of God's Word and for welcoming travelers who shared the gospel. John says word has spread about Gaius' loving-kindness. Then John writes about a man named Diotrephes. John says Diotrephes is a prideful man who wants to lead the church. He has not shown hospitality to Christian travelers and has thrown out of the church those who have taken them into their homes. He is spreading lies and gossip about John and other believers. John says if he comes there, he will show that Diotrephes is not the prominent Christian leader that he thinks he is.

Diotrephes is the perfect example of a prideful gossip. In Romans 1:30, Paul speaks of men like him, men who know God but don't honor Him. "They talk about people, and they hate God. They are filled with pride and tell of all the good they do."

Gossip and pride have been the downfall of many Christians, but those who honor God's Word will be praised.

Lord, let everything I say and do be in agreement with Your Word. Amen.

PERFECTION

Not that I have already obtained all this, or have already arrived at my goal, but I press on to take hold of that for which Christ Jesus took hold of me.

PHILIPPIANS 3:12 NIV

Maria, a barista at a small local coffee shop, was known for creating delicious coffee concoctions for holidays. As February approached, she worked diligently trying to create a Valentine's Day drink that was the perfect mix of sweet and spicy, with notes of dark chocolate and a drop of rose or lavender syrup for a hint of floral. But as hard as she tried, Maria wasn't satisfied that she had made the right blend to brew a perfect cup.

There's a familiar saying: Nobody's perfect. It rings true. No one is perfect except God. Paul wrote that he was trying his best to perfectly follow Jesus but hadn't yet reached his goal—Paul knew that he wouldn't be perfect until He got to heaven. Through salvation, Paul had the promise of all his imperfections being wiped away.

Like Paul, we should keep striving for perfection. By not giving up, we can make our lives a blend of ingredients that although not perfect, will certainly please the Lord.

Dear Jesus, I will do my best to please You as I strive toward perfection in heaven. Amen.

TRUE FAITH

For it is by grace you have been saved, through faith—and this is not from yourselves, it is the gift of God—not by works, so that no one can boast.

EPHESIANS 2:8–9 NIV

Some Christians believe they must work their way into heaven by doing good deeds. Good works are admirable, but it isn't goodness that leads to heaven. Instead, heaven is God's gift to us through faith in Jesus. A path made of good works doesn't lead to heaven, but accepting Jesus as our Lord and Savior does. Through God's grace and our faith in Jesus, we are saved from the punishment of our sins. When we confess that we are sinners and ask Jesus into our hearts, heaven is guaranteed.

About good works, James 2:20 says, "Do you want evidence that faith without deeds is useless?" True faith is transformative. When we are saved, it changes who we are, and we want to serve Jesus by modeling His characteristics of loving-kindness. True faith in Jesus makes us want to do good works, but it is faith that leads us to heaven.

Precious Lord, thank You for Your gift of salvation and the promise of heaven. May others see You through my actions and my words. Amen.

ALL THINGS GOOD AND LOVELY

Your love has given me much joy and comfort.
PHILEMON 1:7 NLV

In Denmark, people enjoy "hygge." It's pronounced "hoo-gah," and it describes anything that makes us feel comfortable and content. It is very hygge, for example, to drink a steaming cup of coffee while reading a good book by the fireplace. A candlelit dinner with your husband is hygge. So is snuggling under a warm blanket while listening to soft music or watching a movie. Hygge is cuddling your child or your pet. It can also be experiencing good times with close friends, celebrating the small joys in life. Hygge is everything comforting and relaxing.

There is a quiet kind of joyfulness that comes with hygge. It is God's love creating a warm glow inside our hearts. Whatever brings us hygge—whether it's quiet time at home, lazy time on the beach, or sharing joyful times with friends, whatever is good and lovely—comes from God. When we experience these things, we should remember to thank God for them.

Bring some hygge into your home today. Create a cozy environment where you can spend time with family, friends, and—most of all—Jesus.

Lord Jesus, thank You for the gifts of comfort and joy, of happy times with friends, and for everything lovely, cozy, and good. Amen.

PERK UP!

Why are you sad, O my soul? Why have you become troubled within me? Hope in God, for I will yet praise Him, my help and my God.

Psalm 42:11 NLV

Have you ever made coffee using a percolator coffeepot? In this brewing method, the heat from the stove burner boils the water and steam pushes it up through a hollow tube to the basket where the grounds are. The lid of the pot disperses the water, saturating the grounds evenly. Then the water seeps back down into the pot. The percolator lid has a little glass knob through which you can see the water perking. The bubbling sounds of perking coffee along with the coffee's savory aroma is a great way to wake up in the morning.

Maybe you've been feeling a little down lately, and you need to perk up. Spend time praising and worshipping the Lord. Praise is like steam traveling up the tube in the coffeepot. It lifts your words to heaven with a sweet aroma that is pleasing to God. Ask Him to lift you up and perk you up so you can enjoy life's blessings.

Dear Jesus, as I lift my praises to You, please lift me up. Open my heart to the joy that surrounds me. Amen.

JESUS EVERY MORNING

Let me hear Your loving-kindness in the morning, for I trust in You. Teach me the way I should go for I lift up my soul to You.

PSALM 143:8 NLV

Father, we thank Thee for the night,
And for the pleasant morning light;
For rest and food and loving care,
And all that makes the world so fair.
Help us to do the things we should,
To be to others kind and good;
In all we do, in work or play,
To love Thee better day by day.

—*Rebecca J. Weston*[11]

It is good first thing in the morning to thank Jesus for His blessings and ask Him to lead us through our day. Making prayer the first thing we do each morning shows Jesus that we prioritize Him above everything else.

Keeping an attitude of prayer all day long sets our minds on Jesus. If we recognize His voice inside our hearts and follow His commands, then (as Rebecca Weston says in her poem) He will help us do the things we should.

Jesus, thank You for this new day. Amen.

[11] Rebecca J. Weston, "Father, We Thank Thee," Sheet Music Timeless Truths Free Online Library | books, accessed March 3, 2025, https://library.timelesstruths.org/music/Father_We_Thank_Thee/.

SLEEPLESS NIGHTS

I will lie down and sleep in peace.
O Lord, You alone keep me safe.
PSALM 4:8 NLV

Tammy was a lawyer. Sometimes, when she was working on an important case, she had trouble sleeping through the night. She tossed and turned, sighed, and groaned. That kept her husband from sleeping too. "Honey," he said, "we have to do something about this."

"I'll go sleep on the sofa," she answered.

"I meant we have to do something about you not sleeping," he told her.

Most of us have had sleepless nights. There are many reasons for lack of sleep, including stress, anxiety, depression, a taxing job, and too much caffeine. Whatever the reason, lying awake all night is irritating for us and sometimes for our husbands.

When David wrote this psalm, he had plenty of stress and worry. He was literally running for his life from men who wanted to kill him. Yet David was able to sleep peacefully by believing the Lord would keep him safe.

Jesus is our answer to sleepless nights. If we can learn to give him all our thoughts and worries at bedtime, we can lie down and sleep in peace. Use Psalm 4:8 as a bedtime prayer.

Dear Lord, I will lie down now and sleep in peace because You alone keep me safe. Amen.

WHEN A SPOUSE DIES

I lie awake. And I feel like a bird alone on the roof.

PSALM 102:7 NLV

A character in a well-known soap opera quoted Psalm 102:7 after her onscreen husband died. Unable to sleep without her husband by her side, she said, "I lie awake. And I feel like a bird alone on a roof."

Some birds, like mourning doves, mate for life. They are loyal and committed to their partners. Sometimes, we'll see one perched by itself on a roof. Its haunting call sounds like a cry to the spouse that death stole away.

The pain of losing a spouse is beyond words. Our lives turn upside down. In an instant, everything changes. We feel like we're standing alone on life's path, not knowing which way to go. But we are never alone. The Lord is with us, especially when we feel a deep sense of loss. Jesus is our friend. He promises to comfort us and lift us off that roof of despair so we can fly again. The road may be long and hard for a while, but the Lord promises to walk with us, talk with us, and lead us to a new and contented way of life.

Lord Jesus, I feel so lost and alone. I need You! Stay with me and help me. Amen.

QUESTIONING GOD

Now that which we see is as if we were looking in a broken mirror. But then we will see everything.

1 Corinthians 13:12 NLV

A kindergarten Sunday school class had been studying the seven days of creation and the fall of man. "If you could ask God just one question," the teacher said, "what would you ask?" Some of the answers were humorous: "When You rested, did You play video games?" "Did You have to climb a ladder to put up the sun, moon, and stars?" "Were Adam and Eve really naked?" Young children are curious to know every little detail, and the literal way they think can lead to some interesting queries.

The questions we ask God are often rhetorical. As adults we ask, "Why did You allow that to happen?" "Why is there so much suffering in the world?" "How long before You answer my prayer?" Throughout the Bible, we read about people questioning God. It's important to note that believers shouldn't question the Lord's authority. Instead, they should desire a deeper understanding of Him.

What would you ask Him today? Trust Him even though you don't have an answer.

Dear Lord, there is much I don't understand about Your ways, but I still trust You. Everything You do somehow leads to something good. Amen.

THE TOLERANT TRAVELER

How good and pleasant it is when God's people live together in unity!

PSALM 133:1 NIV

Vicky's mom had planned a cruise for just the two of them. "A girls' getaway," she called it. As much as Vicky wanted to spend time with her mother, she knew they would be sharing a cabin, and that might be an issue. They had very different ways of doing things, and her mother's ways often irritated Vicky. Besides that, her mother snored! As the trip approached, Vicky prayed that God would help them to get along.

The actress Helen Hayes once said, "When traveling with someone, take large doses of patience and tolerance with your morning coffee."[12] The little habits of others can sometimes irritate us, but it's good to remember that some of our habits might irritate them too. If Vicky kept that in mind as they traveled, the trip with her mom might be more pleasant.

God wants us to get along despite our differences. Getting along is possible with a large dose of patience, tolerance, and understanding. Remember what God says in Isaiah 55:8: "For My thoughts are not your thoughts, neither are your ways my ways."

Jesus, help us all to put aside our differences so we can get along. Amen.

---

[12] "I Can't Believe," *Short North Gazette*, July/August 2019, accessed March 3, 2025, https://www.shortnorth.com/ICan%27tBelieveCurrent.html.

MENTORS

Older women are to teach the young women
to love their husbands and children.
TITUS 2:4 NLV

Maryann cleaned houses on weekends to help supplement her income. Her favorite client was an older woman named Lillian. Well into her eighties, Lillian remained fiercely independent, still living in her home and driving occasionally. While Maryann cleaned, Lillian spent her time reading the Bible. Often, she would ask Maryann a question like, "Did you know, Maryann, that Jesus is the only way to heaven? It says it right here. . ." and then she would read the scripture. As the weeks passed, Maryann began asking Lillian questions about the Bible and Jesus. Their conversations often turned to Maryann's marriage and kids, and Lillian did her best to give the young woman wise, biblical advice.

Older Christian women have experienced a lot of living, and along with it a lot of praying and learning about the Lord. They can be wonderful mentors to younger women who are willing to listen and learn. If you are one of these older women, think about how you can share some of your wisdom with the younger women in your life.

• •

Lord Jesus, thank You for the wisdom of
older Christians. Guide us to learn from them
and share what we've learned. Amen.

THE OLD STAINED CUP

"Come now, let us think about this together," says the Lord. "Even though your sins are bright red, they will be as white as snow. Even though they are dark red, they will be like wool."

ISAIAH 1:18 NLV

Many women have a favorite coffee cup. In some ways, a favorite cup is like a security blanket. We can count on it being there each morning filled with something that makes us feel good. Eventually, though, our favorite coffee cup becomes old and stained. We scrub and scrub, but the stains won't come out. It's tough saying goodbye to that old cup—but it's time.

We've all sinned while knowing it was sin. The Holy Spirit made us feel guilty when we knew our words or behaviors weren't pleasing to God. But we did our best to bury the guilt. We kept on doing those things until finally we said, "Enough!" We took our stained behavior to God and asked Him to forgive us.

The Lord agrees to remove the stains from our lives and give us a brand-new cup. It's our job, though, to keep it clean so it will last a lifetime.

Jesus, thank You for washing away my sins and giving me a new start. Help me keep my behavior clean and pleasing to You. Amen.

MY COFFEE LET ME DOWN

You servants who are owned by someone must obey your owners. Work for them as hard as you can. Work for them the same as if you were working for Christ.

EPHESIANS 6:5 NLV

Susan sat at her desk clutching her coffee mug and staring at her computer. She hadn't shaken off the sleepiness she felt after a restless night. She'd made her coffee extra strong that morning, and the mug was almost empty. "Wake up, Susan!" her boss said cheerfully. "Our meeting starts in five minutes." "I'll wake up as soon as my coffee does," Susan replied. Coffee had let her down that morning, and the last thing she wanted was to sit in a boring meeting trying not to fall asleep.

Paul reminds us in Ephesians 6:5 that we should work as if we are working for Jesus. That means shaking off feelings of sleepiness, boredom, and indifference, and doing our best to serve Him in whatever we do. Could you imagine Jesus saying, "I don't feel like working today"? He is our strength and our model for work. We can overcome our lack of enthusiasm by keeping our minds set on Him.

Dear Jesus, help me to overcome attitudes and feelings that interfere with my work. In everything I do, I want to serve You. Amen.

BUILT ON THE ROCK

A house is built by wisdom. It is made strong by understanding, and by much learning the rooms are filled with all riches that are pleasing and of great worth.

PROVERBS 24:3–4 NLV

In Matthew 7:24–27, Jesus said, "Whoever hears these words of Mine and does them, will be like a wise man who built his house on rock. The rain came down. The water came up. The wind blew and hit the house. The house did not fall because it was built on rock. Whoever hears these words of Mine and does not do them, will be like a foolish man who built his house on sand. The rain came down. The water came up. The wind blew and hit the house. The house fell and broke apart."

Jesus is our rock. He wants to be the foundation of our lives and also our homes. The wise apply His Word at home and teach it to their children. When a family builds its home on the rock, its rooms are filled with understanding, learning, and—most of all—love. Nothing can destroy a home built on obedience to God's Word and the wisdom that comes from Jesus.

Lord Jesus, be our rock and our foundation. Give us wisdom and strengthen our family's bond with You. Amen.

WHY WON'T YOU CHANGE?

Jesus Christ is the same yesterday and today and forever.

HEBREWS 13:8 NLV

"How are things going with Brad?" Evie asked her cousin Mia.

"Not great," said Mia. "I told him if he doesn't change, I'm breaking up with him."

"You can't make him change," Evie said. "It seems like he doesn't want to. Does Brad know the Lord?"

"He says he's a Christian," Mia answered, "but he doesn't act like one. He says one thing and does another."

Evie was right when she advised Mia she couldn't change her boyfriend. Wanting someone to change is a common reason couples break up. Trust is a key element in any relationship, and Mia couldn't trust her boyfriend to be true to his word.

There is one friend we can always trust: Jesus. We can know who Jesus is, what He stands for, and what He expects from us by reading about Him, praying to Him, and strengthening our relationship with Him. Unlike Mia's boyfriend, Jesus will never go back on His Word. He is the same yesterday, today, and forever. When couples make Jesus their foundation, they form a stronger connection with Him and each other.

Dear Lord, guide us to become more like You, to trust You, and to grow nearer to You and one another. Amen.

IN-BETWEEN

Your ears will hear a word behind you, saying, "This is the way, walk in it," whenever you turn to the right or to the left.

ISAIAH 30:21 NLV

We all have in-between times. Times that are status quo and we want something more. Times when we can't decide. Times when our relationship with the Lord, or others, is in between what it was and what we want it to be. In between is the place where we stop, and ask, "What now?"

In the Bible, we often find people who are in between. An example is when the Israelites were in between Egypt and the Promised Land. Forty years they wandered in circles in the desert, not knowing which way to go. They lost patience, turned away from God, cried, wailed, and begged, "Which way?" In His own time, God led them where He wanted them to go.

Patience is the key to navigating our in-between times. The Lord is always faithful. The restlessness we feel in between is the Holy Spirit telling us that God is about to do something. In time, the Lord will say, "This is the way, walk in it." Then He will lead us.

Oh, Lord, I am lost in between. Patiently, I will wait for You to say, "This is the way, walk in it." Amen.

ABANDONED?

God, do not keep quiet; God, do not be silent or still.

Psalm 83:1 NCV

Carrie's pastor made a coffee date with her so they could talk. Carrie had recently confided in her pastor that she felt depressed after her boyfriend left her. As the two women sat in a quiet corner of the coffee shop, Carrie said, "Everyone abandons me. Even God abandoned me. I keep asking Him to fix this, but He's silent. I just move from one bad relationship to another."

"God hasn't abandoned you, Carrie," her pastor said. "Sometimes, He loves us best with silence. Maybe He's silent because He wants you to take a break from getting into another relationship and instead work on your relationship with Him. God doesn't only speak to us by answering our prayers the way we want Him to. He speaks through His Word in the Bible and by closing doors in our lives and opening new ones when He's ready." Carrie's pastor shared with her examples from the Bible when God brought people nearer to Him through His silence—when they couldn't hear His voice, they sought Him.

When God is quiet, He is still with us, teaching us and leading us nearer to Him.

Lord God, when You are silent or still,
teach me. Draw me near as I seek You. Amen.

BITTERSWEET

Pleasing words are like honey. They are sweet to the soul and healing to the bones.

PROVERBS 16:24 NLV

Freshly harvested coffee beans have a bitter taste and are not suitable for eating. Once roasted, the dark-brown beans remain bitter but become edible. Some people enjoy snacking on coffee beans. Confectioners often coat espresso beans in either milk chocolate or dark chocolate, creating a bittersweet flavor and a softer crunch. Coffee enthusiasts appreciate the mocha-like sweetness of chocolate-covered beans, as well as the caffeine boost they provide.

Much like unroasted coffee beans, the words we speak in anger or without thinking can have a bitter quality. Harsh words are difficult to ingest and often remain bitter even after being processed. A heartfelt and sincere apology, however, can help sweeten the bitterness, and adding a touch of forgiveness can aid in healing the soul. The right words, when delivered in the right manner, can truly be a blessing—they are easy to digest, provide comfort, and promote healing.

Take a moment to reflect on the words you've spoken lately. Are there some you need to cover with a sweet coating of kindness, humility, or forgiveness?

Dear Jesus, forgive me for not thinking before I speak. Help me to seek reconciliation from those I've hurt by the harsh words I've said. Amen.

TRUSTED FRIENDS

Then Aaron and Hur held up his hands, one on each side.

EXODUS 17:12 NLV

As the Israelites traveled to the Promised Land an enemy army, the Amalekites, attacked them. Joshua and his men fought them, and meanwhile, Moses, Aaron, and Hur went to the top of a hill and watched. Moses had the special stick God had given him. When Moses held up the stick in his hands, the Israelites were winning. If he put his hands down, the Amalekites won. Exodus 17:12–13 tells us, "Moses' hands became tired. So [Aaron and Hur] took a stone and put it under him, and he sat on it. Then Aaron and Hur held up his hands, one on each side. His hands did not move until the sun went down. So Joshua destroyed Amalek and his people."

Aaron and Hur were Moses' trusted friends. When he chose them to accompany him to the top of the hill, Moses knew they would support him.

We all need Aarons and Hurs in our lives—friends who will rush in to help when we're tired and losing the fight. Who are your Aarons and Hurs?

Lord, thank You for trusted friends who will fight for me when I'm losing the battle and hold me up when I'm weary. Amen.

BODY AND SOUL

"Older people are wise, and long life brings understanding."

Job 12:12 NCV

Our bodies weaken as they age, but as we become older, our wisdom and strength in the Lord grow stronger. As long as we live, God will continue to use us to serve Him. Paul is an example of this. He often spoke about times when his body was afflicted by suffering and pain. Despite these challenges, God gave Paul a strong spirit, enabling him to continue serving even while sick or in prison.

Some people say, "You're as old as you feel." They're not speaking about how your body feels, but your spirit. In our old age, God makes us soul strong. Even if we aren't physically strong, we can still use our wisdom and inner strength to serve. Remember David's words in Psalm 71:18: "Even though I am old and gray, do not leave me, God. I will tell the children about your power; I will tell those who live after me about your might."

"Old" is a state of mind. If you are an older adult, ask God to continue to use you. He's not finished with you here on earth until He calls you home.

Jesus, although my body has aged, my soul is wise and strong. Teach me to use it to serve You. Amen.

FAITH IN THE VALLEY

Yes, even if I walk through the valley of the shadow of death, I will not be afraid of anything, because You are with me.

Psalm 23:4 NLV

When peace, like a river, attendeth my way,
When sorrows like sea billows roll;
Whatever my lot, thou hast taught me to say,
It is well, it is well with my soul.

The words to the hymn "It Is Well with My Soul" were written in 1873 by a devout Christian businessman and lawyer, Horatio G. Spafford. Some of his fortune had been lost in the Great Chicago Fire, and his son had died a short time before. As a respite from their troubles, Spafford planned a European trip for himself, his wife, and their four daughters. Spafford sent his family ahead of him, planning to join them several days later—but then tragedy struck again. The ship sank. Only Mrs. Spafford survived. Horatio wrote the words to his hymn as he sailed to be with her.

Faith in the midst of tragedy is being able to say, "It is well with my soul." Stories like Spafford's remind us that even in the valleys of life, the Lord is with us and faithful.

Lord God, help me build a faith so strong that nothing can get in its way. Amen.

BE REASSURED!

Do not fear, for I am with you. Do not be afraid, for I am your God. I will give you strength, and for sure I will help you. Yes, I will hold you up with My right hand that is right and good.

ISAIAH 41:10 NLV

In a Charles Schulz comic strip, Snoopy lies awake at night atop his doghouse looking worried and afraid. He leaps off his house and rushes to wake Charlie Brown. "Are you upset, little friend?" asks Charlie. He goes on to reassure Snoopy that everything will be okay. He cites Bible examples, "The flood water will recede; the famine will end." He tells Snoopy that he will always be there to care for him. "Be reassured!" Charlie Brown shouts, raising his hand upward toward the sky.[13]

If you lie awake at night worrying about family, jobs, finances, health, floods, famines, or whatever, shift your thoughts to examples in the Bible of God working everything out for good. Isaiah 41:10 is God's reassurance that He is with you. He will strengthen and help you and hold you up—Be reassured! God will take care of you.

Dear Jesus, I sometimes need reassurance of Your constant presence. Remind me of the many times You have helped me, held me up, and strengthened me. Amen.

---

[13] "Peanuts - Jul 18th, 1993 - Comic Art Print," GoComics, January 8, 2025, https://store.gocomics.com/product/pe930718/.

THE BEATITUDES

I will never forget Your Word.

PSALM 119:93 NLV

Most of us have read Jesus' words from the Sermon on the Mount, including the Beatitudes, but how often have we reflected on how we've seen His words play out in our everyday lives? Read them again. See if you find a fresh perspective on the ways God cares for us.

"They are blessed who realize their spiritual poverty,
for the kingdom of heaven belongs to them.
They are blessed who grieve,
for God will comfort them.
They are blessed who are humble,
for the whole earth will be theirs.
They are blessed who hunger and thirst after justice,
for they will be satisfied.
They are blessed who show mercy to others,
for God will show mercy to them.
They are blessed whose thoughts are pure,
for they will see God.
They are blessed who work for peace,
for they will be called God's children.
They are blessed who are persecuted for doing good,
for the kingdom of heaven belongs to them."

MATTHEW 5:3–10 NCV

Lord Jesus, give me a fresh perspective whenever I reread Your words. Amen.

HOW DO YOU MEASURE UP?

Well done, good and faithful servant.

MATTHEW 25:23 KJV

The poet T. S. Eliot wrote, "I have measured out my life with coffee spoons."[14] Imagine if at the end of your life all you had to show for it was how much coffee you drank. Of course, that idea is ludicrous. We measure our lives in years, months, and days, by our successes and failures, and by how many times we've been hurt or we hurt others. We measure by how much we've lost, how much we've gained, and what we've learned. We measure ourselves against people and standards. But there are far better ways to measure.

Ask yourself: How much have I grown in my relationship with the Lord, in faith, trust, and obedience to Him? How much have I become more like Jesus through His teachings and by imitating His character traits? The Lord is surely measuring our lives, but how do we measure up? Measuring our lives by our commitment to Jesus helps us to envision a future in heaven where we can look forward to hearing Him say, "Well done, good and faithful servant."

Dear Jesus, please help me strengthen my faith and trust in You. Guide me to be more devoted to You in everything I do. Amen.

[14] "Prufrock and Other Observations," The Project Gutenberg eBook of Prufrock and Other Observations, by T. S. Eliot, accessed March 3, 2025, https://www.gutenberg.org/files/1459/1459-h/1459-h.htm#linklovesonghttps://www.britannica.com/topic/The-Love-Song-of-J-Alfred-Prufrockhttps://ia801708.us.archive.org/26/items/prufrock_2010_librivox/prufrockandotherobservations_01_eliot_128kb.mp3.

INSTANT COFFEE

I wait for the Lord. My soul waits and I hope in His Word. My soul waits for the Lord more than one who watches for the morning; yes, more than one who watches for the morning.

PSALM 130:5–6 NLV

Yolanda chose a packet of vanilla-flavored instant coffee from the basket on the conference room table. She sprinkled the grounds into her cup, added hot water, and gave it a few stirs. "I wish finding a solution to our problem was as instant as this coffee," she told her coworkers.

We live in a world of instant everything. Instant messaging, instant information, instant notifications, instant potatoes, instant oatmeal, instant coffee. . .gradually, "instant" has stolen our patience. We expect everything to be quick and easy. When it's not, we become restless.

One of the more challenging facets of our relationship with the Lord is waiting for Him to act. Waiting is hard, yet He requires it of us. Waiting means patience, trust, and faith. While we wait, we should spend time in His Word, pray, and remember that God will answer every prayer, and His timing is always perfect.

Dear Jesus, waiting is hard. Every morning I ask, "Is this the day You will answer me?" But yet, I trust You. Your timing is perfect and I know it well. Amen.

UNDERSTANDING IS "RUFF"

Think about these things and the Lord will help you understand them.
2 Timothy 2:7 NLV

If you've ever had a dog, you've probably tried having conversations with them. We talk to our canines as if they are human. They tip their heads to one side, twitch their ears, make noises, and look at us with confused expressions as they struggle to find meaning in a language they don't understand.

For us humans, comprehending God's Word can be equally as challenging. We read the Bible, tilt our heads, furrow our brows, and shake our heads in confusion. We say, "What does this mean? I've read and reread this passage, and I still don't understand it!" It may be that the Lord wants us to dig deeper to understand the meaning of His words. Reading the passage in different translations of the Bible can help. Reading different commentaries can help too. Sometimes, God wants us to stop and think about what we don't understand because there is a personal message in the passage meant just for us.

Paul's words in 2 Timothy 2:7 are a reminder not to disregard scripture that we don't comprehend. Instead, think about His words. Ask Him to help you understand.

Lord, what about this scripture passage do You want me to understand? Enlighten me, please. Amen.

JONAH, ADRIÁN, AND THE WHALE

For with God nothing shall be impossible.
LUKE 1:37 KJV

Jonah ran from God. He sailed away trying to avoid God's command that he go to Nineveh and preach to its people. The ship's crew thought Jonah's disobedience had caused a huge storm that threatened to sink the ship, so they thew Jonah overboard. Just then, God allowed a whale to swallow Jonah. He was trapped in its belly for three days and nights, all the while praying, "I'm worshiping you, GOD, calling out in thanksgiving! And I'll do what I promised I'd do!" (Jonah 2:9 MSG).

Did you think it couldn't happen again? In 2005, Adrián Simancas, a kayaker paddling through the Strait of Magellan, was briefly swallowed by a whale.[15] The first thing he noticed inside its mouth was slime. He desperately thought of how he could survive and escape. Then, as in Jonah's story, the whale spit him out. Adrián didn't say he'd prayed, but he said he had been given a second chance.

Nothing is impossible with God. History often repeats itself. Our God is the God of all things possible and the God of second chances.

Dear Lord, with You nothing is impossible. What You've done in the past, You can do again. Thank You for Your daily mercies and steadfast love. Amen.

---

[15] Andrea Díaz & Ayelén Oliva. "'I felt a slimy texture brush my face': Man describes being swallowed by whale," *BBC*, February 14, 2025, https://www.bbc.com/news/articles/cly50k8zypmo

LOST IN THE CLUTTER

Jesus said to her, "Martha, Martha, you are worried and troubled about many things. Only a few things are important, even just one. Mary has chosen the good thing. It will not be taken away from her."

Luke 10:41–42 NLV

Jesus visited His friends Mary and Martha. Mary sat near Jesus listening to everything He said while Martha prepared their meal. In Luke 10:40 Martha became irritated and said to Jesus, "Do You see that my sister is not helping me? Tell her to help me." Jesus responded by telling her that she was worried about the wrong things, but "Mary has chosen the good thing."

Whether we like it or not, our lives are filled with clutter. Your purse is filled with clutter. Your kitchen table might be cluttered with mail and your sink with dishes. Your mind can be cluttered with a million things to do, and your time spent trying to get them done. Jesus reminds us that nothing is more important than prioritizing Him. He can get lost in the clutter when our to-do lists are long and our minds are filled with worry. Make Jesus your priority. See that He is always first on your list.

Jesus, please forgive me for not making You my first priority. Amen.

DIAL 3-3-3

"Call to Me, and I will answer you. And I will show you great and wonderful things which you do not know."

JEREMIAH 33:3 NLV

Bev picked up the call to hear her sister's raspy voice. "We need to cancel our plans. I have a sore throat, my body aches, and my nose is running."

"Do you need anything?" Bev asked.

"No, just rest."

"Call me if you need me," said Bev. "Love you, and don't forget to dial 3-3-3."

It was something their mother had said when they were children, "Dial 3-3-3." It was her way of telling them to pray about their problems. Jeremiah 33:3 says, "Call to Me, and I will answer you. And I will show you great and wonderful things which you do not know."

How comforting it is to be confident that whenever we need Him, the Lord will pick up our call. He is like a telehealth doctor, always ready, always there 24-7. The Lord is ready to help us solve problems, make decisions, provide comfort when we are sick or sad, or just talk for a while.

If you need anything, dial 3-3-3. Jesus is waiting to answer your call.

Dear Jesus, I'm comforted knowing You will pick up my calls all day and all night. I love You. Amen.

GOD LOVES YOU!

In him and through faith in him we may approach God with freedom and confidence.

EPHESIANS 3:12 NIV

The adult Sunday school class discussed the meaning of "fear the Lord" found in scripture. They spoke of being reverent and obedient to Him and of being in awe of His power and greatness. One woman said, "I've always been afraid of God. When we were little, our mother told us that God saw the naughty things we did, and He was going to punish us. I imagined Him like the great and mighty wizard in *The Wizard of Oz*."

"It's true that God is mighty in power," an older gentleman responded. "He hates evil and promises to destroy it, but God is also love. Through faith in Jesus, all your sins—past, present, and future—are forgiven. Jesus took the punishment you deserved. So you shouldn't be afraid of Him. God loves you."

How great is God's love! He loves us so much that He allowed His own Son to be punished in our place. We can approach God with freedom and confidence, without any fear, assured that He will respond with gentle kindness and forgiveness. Don't ever forget how much He loves you.

Lord God, I honor and respect You, and I'm grateful every day for Your perpetual kindness and love. Amen.

ABOVE THE DIN

"See! I stand at the door and knock. If anyone hears My voice and opens the door, I will come in to him and we will eat together."

REVELATION 3:20 NLV

Mom is in the kitchen making a smoothie in the blender. In the garage, dad is sawing two-by-fours with his power saw. The volume on the TV in the living room is turned up high, and their teenage son is practicing his drums upstairs. Someone is knocking at the door, but no one hears. What if it were Jesus knocking? What if He had come hoping to visit with you today?

We can become so preoccupied with noisy thoughts and distractions that we can't hear Jesus knocking at the door to our hearts. We may have welcomed Him in the first time, when we accepted Him as our Savior. But every day since, Jesus has continued to knock, saying, "Please let me in. I want to help you today. I want to talk with you, teach you, strengthen and encourage you." Sometimes, we don't open the door because we can't hear above the world's constant din. Listen. Is Jesus knocking? Stop what you're doing and let Him in.

Above the din, I can hear You knocking. Come in, Lord Jesus. Come in. Amen.

A JOYFUL GOOD MORNING

This is the day that the Lord has made.
Let us be full of joy and be glad in it.
Psalm 118:24 NLV

Good morning! Did you wake up refreshed and feeling glad? If you did, wonderful! This is the day the Lord has made. Enjoy the beauty that surrounds you. Be grateful and filled with joy. But maybe you didn't wake up feeling great. Maybe something is happening today that you aren't looking forward to. As much as we want to be joyful and glad every day, some days we just aren't.

David, author of today's scripture verse, had plenty of bad days. But even on his darkest days, David praised the Lord. Perhaps he focused on whatever good he could find in each day. He was alive. God kept him safe from his enemies. When afraid, David found comfort knowing God would fight for him, and he slept peacefully believing God was with him. David found joy simply by having a relationship with the Lord.

With Jesus by our side, we can find gladness and joy every day by focusing on His blessings. Ask Jesus to fill your heart with the joy of knowing Him.

Good morning, dear Jesus. Thank You for this day.
Walk with me. Talk with me and fill my heart with joy. Amen.

SECRET MENU

"I will give you hidden treasures, riches stored in secret places, so that you may know that I am the Lord, the God of Israel, who summons you by name."

Isaiah 45:3 NIV

Sheila and her daughter Tiffany were on their way to try out a new drive-through coffee place. As her mother drove, Tiffany was busy scrolling through her phone. "Hey. They have a secret menu!" she exclaimed. "Check this out. You can get flavors like Green Gummy Bear, Birthday Cake, and Cherry Cobbler. I'm getting the Firecracker latte—it's made with cayenne pepper, white chocolate, and cinnamon." Going online and finding a restaurant's secret menu is like finding a hidden treasure. It's unearthing something wonderful that others might not know about.

God hides little treasures all around us. We might get a glimpse of the Northern Lights or see a dolphin leap out of the ocean. It could be finding something we'd misplaced long ago or receiving a surprise gift from someone. Have you ever experienced something special and unexpected and said, "I know that was You, God!"? Never stop looking for God's secret menu. It's there, just waiting for you to find it.

Lord, what wonderful things have You hidden that You want me to find? Open my eyes so I can see them. Amen.

THE AMBASSADOR CAFÉ

We are therefore Christ's ambassadors, as though God were making his appeal through us.
2 Corinthians 5:20 NIV

Around the corner from a small community college is a little coffee shop named the Ambassador Café. On the outside, its brick facade looks like any other quaint coffee shop, but inside something special—and wonderful—is happening. It's not about the wireless internet or the colorful, funky artwork on the walls, and it isn't about the coffee either, although it's the best! The café is known for having a Bible on each table, scripture verses written on its coffee cups, and a spunky barista named Pearl who hosts Tuesday night karaoke where patrons sing worship songs.

The Bible instructs us to be ambassadors for Christ. Some Christians use their creative ideas to spread the gospel and tell others about Jesus. The Ambassador Café is a good example. Its owners found a way for patrons to come in wanting coffee and leave thinking about Jesus. The Holy Spirit inspires us with unique ways to act as Christ's ambassadors. How can you be an ambassador for Him?

Dear Jesus, show me how I can use my creativity to share Your story with others. Guide me to share the gospel in unique and exciting ways. Amen.

HEART TO HEART

God has given each of you a gift. Use it to help each other. This will show God's loving-favor.

1 Peter 4:10 NLV

Each of us has talents and skills given to us by God. Some have the gift of music, painting, textile art, writing, acting, dancing, or photography. Others are blessed with the gift of listening, comforting, caregiving, encouraging, teaching, or leading. All our special gifts require imagination to generate ideas. Each is an art. The gifts God gives us are diverse, and the ways we use them are unique.

Aristotle is credited with saying, "The aim of art is to represent not the outward appearance of things, but their inward significance." Our gifts come from the heart, and we can use them to reach the hearts of others. They can bring joy, soothe sadness and suffering, encourage, inspire, instruct—the list goes on. There are as many ways to use our gifts as there are ideas. The Bible tells us to use our gifts to help each other. How we use them comes from the heart.

Think of how the skills and talents of others have been a blessing to you and how yours can be a blessing.

Dear Jesus, inspire me to use my special gifts to touch the hearts of others. Amen.

PEOPLE PLEASERS

Am I now trying to win the approval of human beings, or of God? Or am I trying to please people? If I were still trying to please people, I would not be a servant of Christ.

GALATIANS 1:10 NIV

"What's going on?" Jim asked his wife. "You seem angry."

"I am," said Grace. "I'm always giving to others and saying 'yes' to what everyone wants, but I feel like my wants and needs don't matter." Grace went on to tell her husband about helping a friend. "When I left," Grace said. "All I got was, 'Thanks, Grace. I appreciate you.'"

"What more did you expect?" asked Jim.

Grace is a people pleaser. People pleasers are motivated by needing approval from others. Not receiving it leaves them feeling unfulfilled, resentful, and even angry. The opposite of people pleasers is those who are motivated by wanting to please God. They reach out with acts of kindness, expecting nothing in return.

It is good to do some self-examination to determine who we are serving and what we expect to receive. Paul says in Galatians 1:10 that if our motivation is trying to win the approval of others, we aren't authentic servants of Christ.

Lord, guide me to be Your servant by helping others, expecting nothing in return. The only approval I seek is Yours. Amen.

SERVANTS OF CHRIST

"Does the servant get thanks for doing what he was told to do? I am sure he does not. It is the same with you also. When you do everything you have been told to do, you must say, 'We are not any special servants. We have done only what we should have done.'"

LUKE 17:9–10 NLV

The word *servant* conjures images of medieval castles, cooks, butlers, chambermaids, thankless jobs, and low pay. Perhaps the only bonus was having a room in the castle.

When the Bible speaks of being a servant of Christ, the word has an entirely different meaning. Jesus' servants choose to serve Him because they love Him. His servants do everything they are told because they trust Him. They obey and try to please Him because He treats them well. Jesus' servants don't think of themselves as greater than those who serve kings and queens. They are humble, like Jesus, sacrificing their own needs for the needs of others. They serve without thanks or pay, and instead of a room in a castle, they look forward to a mansion in heaven.

Our lives are tremendously fulfilling when we serve our Master, Jesus Christ, the Lord.

Dear Jesus, I am honored to serve You, and I will do my best to serve You well. Amen.

BEGGING FOR CAFFEINE

To this end I strenuously contend with all the energy Christ so powerfully works in me.

COLOSSIANS 1:29 NIV

Gianna works as a fire lookout in a national forest. She says it's one of the loneliest jobs in the world. During fire season, she ascends the tower to a tiny room where she sits watching over acres of land through her binoculars. On the night shift, her body begs for caffeine to stay alert. She knows she can't fall asleep. Early detection of a fire is vital.

In Colossians 1:28–29, Paul writes about needing to warn people of the danger of not knowing Christ. Paul understands his work is crucial. His body is struggling, but Paul knows Jesus will give him power to carry on. Whatever Paul does, he works with energy, enthusiasm, and clear understanding, as if working for the Lord.

We all struggle against sleep—staying up with a sick baby, driving cross country, working at a solitary job like Gianna's. When an important task requires staying alert and focused, we often need the caffeine from coffee to keep us going. However, even more than that, we need Jesus.

Lord God, whenever I have an important task to complete and I feel weary, please provide me with the energy to stay alert and perform my job well. Amen.

THE JITTERS

When anxiety was great within me,
your consolation brought me joy.
PSALM 94:19 NIV

We love coffee because it tastes good. We also rely on coffee to help us stay awake and alert. Coffee's caffeine is a natural stimulant, but too much can give us shaky hands, a racing heart, and an overall nervous feeling called "the jitters." The cure? Cut back on the caffeine.

Worry and stress cause jitters too. It's the unpleasant feeling of anticipation before we go for a job interview, take a test, or give a speech. Usually, the feeling goes away. But sometimes, anxiety stays with us, triggering an attitude of readiness and an underlying sensation that something bad is about to happen. The cure is to cut back on the worry and trust Jesus. He says, "Learn the unforced rhythms of grace. I won't lay anything heavy or ill-fitting on you. Keep company with me and you'll learn to live freely and lightly" (Matthew 11:30 MSG).

Give your anxiety and worries to Jesus today. Letting them go will open your heart to feelings of consolation and joy that only He can give.

Oh, Lord, please help me to release these feelings of anxiety and worry. I know that You are bigger than my problems and that You will care for me and keep me safe. Amen.

STIRRING THOUGHTS

You will show me the way of life. Being with You is to be full of joy. In Your right hand there is happiness forever.
Psalm 16:11 NLV

Bob and Marie sat at their kitchen table looking at photos and reminiscing about a trip they'd made to the Holy Land many years before. "That trip was great," Marie said wistfully. "Bethlehem, the shepherds' fields, the Sea of Galilee, Via Dolorosa. It stirs so many thoughts in me and even more questions. I wish we could go back."

"I do too," said Bob. "The Lord showed us many things while we were there, and we learned so much."

It's fun to reminisce about vacations and think of what we saw and learned. But we don't have to travel for Jesus to show us new and exciting things. We find them in the Bible as He reveals new meanings and fresh understanding. We see them in loving-kindness all around us. The Lord stirs our thoughts, causes us to question, and makes us want to learn more about Him. He is stirring your thoughts right now, wanting to show you the joy of being with Him. So follow Jesus. Discover where He and your thoughts take you.

Jesus, turn my thoughts toward You.
Walk with me and show me the way of life. Amen.

ONE LITTLE TOWN

"Bethlehem Ephrathah. . .from you One will come who will rule for Me in Israel. His coming was planned long ago, from the beginning."

MICAH 5:2 NLV

How well do you know the Bible?

What did God tell Micah about where the Messiah would be born? (Micah 5:2)

Where did Rachel die? (Genesis 35:19)

What was the name of Naomi's hometown? (Ruth 1)

Where did King David spend his early childhood? (1 Samuel 17:12)

To which city did Mary and Joseph travel for the census? (Luke 2:4)

Where was Jesus born? (Luke 2:6)

If you answered these correctly, you would notice all the answers are the same.

Bethlehem is a little town, but not too little to be connected to Bible greats like Rachel, Naomi, David, and of course Jesus. Much has changed since Bible times. Bethlehem is located today in the West Bank of Palestine. This place where hope began is rife with trouble. But its history still stands. One day, Jesus will return to this area, and then hope will become reality.

Jesus, protect Bethlehem, the place of Your birth. Keep hope alive there until Your return. Amen.

GOING TO SEE THE RABBITS

If one gives an answer before he hears,
it makes him foolish and ashamed.
PROVERBS 18:13 NLV

Elaine Williamson taught first grade at a Christian school in Iowa. Her class was learning proper nouns by naming cities. When a student named a city, Elaine showed it on a map. "My grandma lives in Des Moines!" "We used to live in Milwaukee!" "We're going to See the Rabbits!"

"Tyler," Elaine replied, "*rabbit* is a noun, but today we're looking for proper nouns, names of cities." Then she moved on.

Tyler was clearly disappointed. "But aren't we going to find it on the map?" he said.

The next morning, Tyler was the first one in the classroom. He held a note in his chubby little fist. "Read this!" he said. "We're going to See the Rabbits!" Elaine unfolded the note and read: *Dear Mrs. Williamson, Friday, October 15, will be Tyler's last day in class. We are moving to Cedar Rapids.*

"Oh, Tyler," she said. "You were right. You *are* going to Cedar Rapids!"

Elaine learned to be more patient when she didn't understand. Misunderstood words can cause disappointment and hurt feelings, so it's wise to listen attentively and think before we speak.

Dear Jesus, help me to listen carefully when others speak and do my best to understand. Amen.

THE ART OF KEEPING YOUR COOL

God's servant must not be argumentative, but a gentle listener and a teacher who keeps cool, working firmly but patiently with those who refuse to obey.

2 Timothy 2:24 MSG

Children are often misunderstood. What they think and say can make total sense in their young minds, but it might come across differently to adults. The words Paul wrote in today's scripture weren't specifically meant for parents, but they still hit home. Instead of arguing with our little ones when we aren't sure if they're being stubborn or disagreeable, we should keep our cool and listen patiently while trying to get at what they really mean. Keeping our cool isn't always easy, especially if we are busy, stressed, or in a hurry. But by doing so, we can avoid confrontations, misunderstandings, and all those tears.

Jesus was a gentle, patient listener. Although He already knew what someone thought before they said it, He listened without disregard. Jesus was firm when needed, but He never lost His cool. He used every opportunity to teach. When parenting, Jesus is your best example. Learn from Him to focus on what your children want and need.

Lord Jesus, please remind me to listen carefully to my children and be patient and understanding, especially when I'm busy, stressed out, or in a rush. Amen.

LOOK TO THE SKY

The heavens are telling of the greatness of God and the great open spaces above show the work of His hands.

PSALM 19:1 NLV

Leah proudly displayed her paintings and fabric art on the walls of her coffee shop. Her artistic talent extended to her coffee as a latte artist extraordinaire. Leah found inspiration in nature, especially the sky. She was a master at pouring celestial designs. Patrons oohed and aahed over the swirling clouds, planets, suns, moons, and stars she created on the coffee's surface.

The sky has inspired artists for centuries. A classic example is Vincent van Gogh's *The Starry Night*. In a letter to his brother, he wrote: "It does me good to do what's *difficult*. That doesn't stop me having a tremendous need for. . .religion—so I go outside at night to paint the stars, and I always dream a painting like that."[16] When God created the sky and everything in it, was it to inspire our imaginations? We look up at what we can see and ponder what might lie beyond.

Go outside and look up. See the greatness of God. Praise Him and be inspired by the work of His hands.

Lord, the heavens proclaim Your mighty power. I see it in the sun, moon, and stars. Amen.

[16] "691," 691 (695, 543): To Theo van Gogh. Arles, on or about Saturday, 29 September 1888. Vincent van Gogh Letters, accessed March 3, 2025, https://vangoghletters.org/vg/letters/let691/letter.html.

GIVE IT YOUR BEST SHOT

Everyone should look at himself and see how he does his own work. Then he can be happy in what he has done. He should not compare himself with his neighbor.

GALATIANS 6:4 NLV

Shannon's goal was to become a world champion latte artist. When she thought she was ready, she applied to a well-known, world-class competition. She was thrilled to be accepted. The competition involved a face-to-face match with another latte artist, each producing one drink for the judges to score. The winner moved on to the next round; the loser was eliminated. When Shannon was defeated in the third round, the thrill of being accepted to compete turned to deep disappointment. Comparing herself to the others, Shannon decided she would never compete again.

Comparing our work to what others do can lead to feelings of inadequacy and defeat, or it can lead to learning and becoming better. There is a saying, "If at first you don't succeed, try, try again." Whatever your goal, don't let comparisons get you down. Learn from them and keep trying.

Jesus, please help me be the best I can be without comparing myself to others. You know the way to my goal. Lead me, and I will follow. We will get there together. Amen.

2+2+2

Two are better than one, because they have good pay for their work.

ECCLESIASTES 4:9 NLV

When Pastor John asked Liz to plan a fun field trip for the kids attending vacation Bible school, she panicked. The idea of taking fifty kids of varying ages on a field trip was daunting. "I'll help," said a woman working in the church office. "Count me in," said the pastor's wife, who had stopped by to bring him lunch. A few more women joined in, and the group of six came up with a great idea for an outing for kids of all ages. When the kids found out about the plan, they thought it was a great idea too.

Some tasks are impossible to do alone. We need another person to sing a duet, for example, or to waterski, hug, run a race, or move a piano. The Bible says two are better than one. Since that day when God said Adam needed a helper, people have joined together as helpmates. Teamwork brings us closer together and teaches us to encourage and support one another. It helps us build patience and tolerance, and best of all, helping each other often leads to deep and lasting friendships.

Lord, thank You for placing in my life people whom I can count on for help. Amen.

ONE BIG FAMILY

God promised to give the world to him and to all his family after him. He did not make this promise because Abraham obeyed the Law. He promised to give the world to Abraham because he put his trust in God. This made him right with God.

ROMANS 4:13 NLV

Abraham was very old, and he had no children. In Genesis 15:5, God told Abraham to go outside and look at the stars, and He promised him, "Your children and your children's children will be as many as the stars." He promised to give the world to Abraham and his children, not because of Abraham's obedience but because of his faith.

In Jewish tradition, Abraham is the father of Judaism. But Abraham's descendants aren't just those who share his DNA. Paul says in Galatians 3:29, "If you belong to Christ, then you have become the true children of Abraham." Christians don't connect to Abraham through DNA but instead through trust in Jesus. Everyone who trusts Him as their Savior is adopted into the family of God and becomes an heir to His kingdom and eternal life. Through Jesus' gift of salvation, we become one big family—sisters and brothers in Christ.

Dear Jesus, thank You for making us a family, heirs to Your kingdom, and assured of eternal life in heaven. Amen.

THE WAY HOME

O Lord, I know that a man's way is not known by himself. It is not in man to lead his own steps.

JEREMIAH 10:23 NLV

The assignment was for kids to choose a buddy, pretend they were a GPS, and tell their buddy how they got home from school using street names and specific directions. The buddy's job was to trace the route on a map and find where his friend lived. The assignment was easy for most in the class except for one pair, Aaron and Sam. The line on Sam's map wove through a maze of twists and turns, reached a dead end, and made a U-turn. "Aaron," said their teacher. "Why are you giving Sam such complicated directions?" "Because," Aaron replied, "it *is* complicated. I take the bus, and my house is last on the route."

Our lives are sometimes as complicated as Aaron's directions. We get lost in a labyrinth of unfamiliar paths, unable to find our way home. Proverbs 16:9 says, "The mind of a man plans his way, but the Lord shows him what to do." As Christians, we needn't worry about finding our way home, because the Lord promises to guide us. When we allow Him to lead the way, we are never lost.

Lord, walk through life with me, and lead me home. Amen.

RENEWING OUR VOWS

The king stood by the pillar and renewed the covenant in the presence of the LORD—to follow the LORD and keep his commands, statutes and decrees with all his heart and all his soul.

2 KINGS 23:3 NIV

To celebrate their fiftieth wedding anniversary, Henry and Dorothy traveled across the country to visit the church where they had been married. The little brown church in the valley looked the same as it had all those years before. The couple asked the church pastor if he would lead them in renewing their vows on the church steps. Afterward, the pastor invited them to ring the church bell, signifying the renewal of their vows. Wedding vows are a covenant, a binding agreement to honor and be true to each other with all our heart and soul, until death we part. Dorothy and Henry renewed their vows as a way of reaffirming their love and commitment to one another.

When we commit our lives to Jesus, we enter into a covenant with God. We become one with Him through His forgiveness of our sins. Salvation is the greatest gift and one we should celebrate. Will you stand in the Lord's presence this morning and renew your commitment to honor Him?

Heart and soul, O Lord,
I recommit my life to You. Amen.

OUR TRADITIONS

"When your children ask you, 'Why are we doing these things?' you will say, 'This is the Passover sacrifice to honor the LORD. When we were in Egypt, the LORD passed over the houses of Israel, and when he killed the Egyptians, he saved our homes.'"

EXODUS 12:26–27 NCV

Most Christian families have holiday traditions that honor the Lord—a nativity set to remember His birth, Easter lilies symbolizing Christ's resurrection, family members saying what they are thankful for before their Thanksgiving meal. Family traditions are widely varied and often unique. If our children ask, "Why are we doing this?" it is a great opportunity to use Bible stories to teach them about Jesus.

Traditions are a part of a family's unique identity. Many traditions are handed down from generation to generation. Grandma's cookie recipe, Uncle Ted's special way of dyeing Easter eggs, Mom's tried-and-true way of roasting the Thanksgiving turkey. Our traditions help strengthen our family's bond, and finding ways to connect them with Jesus helps to strengthen our bond with Him. Even if your children don't ask, "Why are we doing these things?" use your traditions to talk about Jesus and lead your children to know Him.

Lord Jesus, show me ways that our family's traditions can guide my children to know and love You. Amen.

IT WILL BE FINE

"Give in to God, come to terms with him and everything will turn out just fine."

JOB 22:21 MSG

Every November, Rita worried about cooking the Thanksgiving turkey. Her husband, Joe, did his best to encourage her by reminding her of how many turkeys she had cooked over the years.

"Rita, we've been married twenty-five years, and you've made twenty-five turkeys. It'll be fine."

"Rita, we've been married forty years, and you've made forty turkeys. . ."

"Rita, we've been married fifty years. . ."

Rita prayed over each turkey, "Dear God, thank You for this turkey. Now please help me to cook it just right so it won't be dry. Amen." She checked the bird often for brownness and juiciness, and when it was done, she'd bring it to the table and say, "I hope it's okay." Joe would announce the annual turkey number, proclaim that the bird was fine, and sit down with the family to eat.

For decades, Rita had experienced God's faithfulness in providing her with a perfect turkey. Still, she continued to worry. God is always faithful. When we learn to trust Him fully, then we don't need to worry. Everything will turn out just fine.

Dear Jesus, forgive me for doubting Your faithfulness. Help me to trust You completely. Amen.

HIS GRACE

But he said to me, "My grace is sufficient for you, for my power is made perfect in weakness."

2 Corinthians 12:9 NIV

How is it that life can get so messy? One word leads to a disagreement, one misstep leads to a fall, and one mistake leads to disaster. One wrong step and we're knee-deep in messiness. We try to get out but fail. Battling the mess, we realize that it's bigger than we are, and we're too weak to fight it and win. We're sinking fast. We have to choose: Will we give up, or will we give it to God?

Giving up is a dismal decision. It means we've lost all hope. The right choice is giving it to God. He will extend His grace to us. Although we've messed up, the Lord will get us out of the mess. His power is made perfect in our weakness, and His gift of forgiveness and loving-kindness is free. It only requires taking our troubles to Him and trusting in His power.

Maybe your life is a little messy right now. Give the mess to Jesus. Ask Him to help you, then trust that He will.

Lord Jesus, I'm caught in a tangled mess, but You know the way out. Please help me. Amen.

IT'S A MIRACLE!

Many people followed him because they saw the miracles he did to heal the sick.

John 6:2 NCV

A recently retired couple, Nora and John, were exploring a new hobby: genealogy. After supper one night, they sat at the kitchen table drinking coffee and searching online for hidden secrets about their ancestors.

"My dad was born in 1918, when there was a terrible flu epidemic," said Nora. "It says here that millions of people died. I remember my grandma saying that Dad had the flu when he was a little baby, and he almost didn't make it."

"And didn't your mom have the measles when she was a kid and almost die?" asked John.

Nora nodded and was silent for a bit. She looked up from her tablet and said, "I guess it's a miracle I'm here."

Each one of us is a miracle created by God, and if we unearth our family history, we will discover more miracles. We will see how the Lord moved us forward generation by generation on the heels of His grace. Think about that today and thank God that you're here. It's a miracle!

Lord God, thank You for protecting and healing my ancestors, which has led me to be here today. Thank You for Your many miracles that have spanned generations. Amen.

PLAIN VANILLA

The people went among the trees and saw honey flowing, but no man tasted it.

1 SAMUEL 14:26 NLV

I scream, you scream, we all scream for ice cream.

Those song lyrics, written in the early 1900s by Howard Johnson, still ring true today. We all scream for ice cream—at least, most of us do. Some ice cream connoisseurs search for the perfect flavor. No plain vanilla for them! They want chili chocolate, guava mint, lemon licorice, or pumpkin cappuccino. Boring old vanilla? No, thank you. Still, among all the diverse and ever-evolving ice cream flavors, vanilla is the most popular.

Have you ever thought that we Christians can act like ice cream addicts hunting for the flavor of our dreams? We pray to God, desperately asking for the perfect answer to our problems, when maybe God's answer is plain-vanilla trust in Jesus. Jesus' message to us is pure and simple: "Trust Me." He knows that the world is giving us all kinds of recipes for solving our problems. Some of them taste good, but none are as good as trust in Jesus.

If you are searching for the perfect answer to your problems today, give plain-vanilla trust a try. You'll be glad that you did.

Jesus, my trust is in You is plain, simple, and solid. Amen.

THE CHICKEN OR THE EGG?

Then God made the wild animals of the earth after their kind, and the cattle after their kind, and every thing that moves upon the ground after its kind. And God saw that it was good.

GENESIS 1:25 NLV

Which came first, the chicken or the egg? It's a question that humans have pondered for years. Some evolutionists believe the egg came first. An egg from a nonchicken mutated into an egg that produced a barnyard chicken. On the other hand, Christians believe that the chicken came first. Proof is in Genesis 1:25.

Although they know better, Christians sometimes put the egg before the chicken. Similar to children eager to discover what treasures are hidden in plastic Easter eggs, they think more about God's gifts than the one who put them there. Without God's gift of salvation through Christ Jesus, and without His gifts of forgiveness and mercy and love, there would be no Resurrection Sunday and no promise of eternal life. There would be no secular reason for cute stuffed chicks, plastic eggs, or the Easter Bunny. We don't need to ask which came first, the chicken or the egg? We know who came first—it was God.

Lord God, Creator of the universe, Thank You for Your endless and immeasurable gifts. Amen.

LAUGH A LITTLE

A glad heart is good medicine,
but a broken spirit dries up the bones.
PROVERBS 17:22 NLV

Pastor Cal poured himself a cup of coffee from the pot in the church office. "Hey, Joyce," he said to the church secretary, "how did Paul make his coffee?"

She smiled, rolled her eyes, and said, "Hebrewed it."

"Aw, you already knew that one," said the pastor. Cal was working on a sermon about God's sense of humor.

Think about the humorous things we find in the Bible. There's Joshua and his men marching 'round and 'round Jericho, looking like fools. There's Balaam with his talking donkey. And the big fish throwing up Jonah, and whatever else was in its stomach, onto the shore. In Proverbs, we find lighthearted sayings such as the one in 22:13: "The lazy man says, 'There is a lion outside!' " (Now, there's an excuse for not mowing the lawn!) God's sense of humor can bring a little laughter into our lives.

The next time you grumble a little too much or have one of those days when nothing goes right, open your eyes and your heart to God, and watch for His perfectly timed sense of humor.

Dear Jesus, today I find myself in need of a little joy and laughter. Please help me see the humorous moments that surround me. Amen.

MOUNTAIN CLIMBING

For He will tell His angels to care for you and keep you in all your ways. They will hold you up in their hands. So your foot will not hit against a stone.

Psalm 91:11–12 NLV

The word *mountain* appears more than five hundred times in the Bible. Mountains symbolize God's greatness. Who else could create something so magnificent? Maybe that's why God chose a mountain setting to deliver some of His most important messages to mankind.

A mountaintop appears as a wonderful place providing an outstanding view, but be careful, it could be an illusion. Matthew 4:8–10 (NIV) says, "The devil took [Jesus] to a very high mountain and showed him all the kingdoms of the world and their splendor. 'All this I will give you,' he said, 'if you will bow down and worship me.'" Make sure you are standing with God on the mountaintop instead of bowing down to Satan. The devil is the master of tricks. He can make evil things appear beautiful, and he wants you to trip and fall down the mountain into a pit of despair. Don't allow it! Be brave and know that God is with you. He will hold you up and not let you fall.

Jesus, help me discern between what is truly lovely and the beautiful side of evil. Amen.

FEAR OF HEIGHTS

The LORD *God is my strength, and he will make my feet like hinds' feet, and he will make me to walk upon mine high places.*

HABAKKUK 3:19 KJV

Maybe you are facing a mountain so high you can't begin to climb it. With feet firmly planted on level ground, you shudder knowing it is a mountain you have to climb. But you're still afraid.

In Hannah Hurnard's classic novel *Hinds' Feet on High Places*, the main character, Much-Afraid (an orphan and lost soul), climbs a mountain hoping to get help from the Good Shepherd (God). She encounters many challenges and obstacles along the way, but with some help, she reaches the mountaintop and sees life from a new perspective. The frightened girl who lacked human love is transformed by God's love into a beautiful, joyful being.

You can be like Much-Afraid and overcome your fear of the high places with faith and God's love. Take that first step. God will provide you with His strength to get past any obstacles. He will stay with you, making sure you don't get lost. He will lead you to the mountaintop, where life is renewed and you can see all the way to eternity.

Lord God, take away my fear and give me strength. Lead me to the mountaintop. Amen.

MR. ETERNITY

"God, have pity on me! I am a sinner!"

LUKE 18:13 NLV

Imagine someone writing the word "Eternity" in chalk on sidewalks more than a half a million times over thirty-seven years. He was an Australian man named Arthur Malcolm Stace. Arthur came from a troubled home. As an adult he was jailed for drunkenness, lost a succession of jobs, and was homeless. Then one night, he wandered into a prayer meeting where he knew he could get a cup of tea and some cake. At that meeting, Arthur admitted his sins and accepted Jesus as his Savior. He later heard a pastor say, "I wish I could shout 'Eternity!' through the streets of Sydney!" So for almost forty years, chalk in hand, Stace wrote "Eternity" all over Sydney. He was the anonymous "Eternity Man," a mysterious street character who remained anonymous for thirty-seven years until finally he was caught in the act. When he died, Arthur left his life savings to missions and his body to science to help those who were sick.[17]

Arthur's life had changed when he met the real Mr. Eternity: Jesus Christ. Jesus changes the lives of all those who know Him, and He uses their lives for good.

Jesus, please forgive my sins and use me to do Your work here on earth. Amen.

---

17 "Shirley Fitzgerald. "Stace, Arthur Malcolm," *State Library: New South Wales*, 2008, https://dictionaryofsydney.org/entry/stace_arthur#ref-uuid=c9dd73f5-cb96-486f-5e1e-0680e841a550

A MULTITUDE OF SINS

If we say that we have no sin, we lie to ourselves and the truth is not in us. If we say we have not sinned, we make God a liar. And His Word is not in our hearts.

1 John 1:8, 10 NLV

Some species of snails are hermaphrodites and can reproduce on their own. Aquarium owners know that if even one snail egg gets into an aquarium, soon dozens of tiny snails will creep along the gravel bottom and up and down the aquarium glass. If they don't get rid of them, soon there will be a multitude of snails.

If you think about it, sin is a lot like snails. If you don't get rid of it right away, it multiplies. God knew this from the beginning. He understood that He had to do something desperate to get rid of our sin once and for all, and His answer was Jesus.

The Bible says that everyone is guilty of sin. We can disguise sin with good intentions, but no matter how much we try to get rid of it, sin will continue to trouble us as long as we live. Isn't it wonderful that Jesus came into the world to save us?

Lord Jesus, thank You for saving me from a multitude of sins. Amen.

COVER SIN WITH LOVE

Above all, love each other deeply,
because love covers over a multitude of sins.

1 PETER 4:8 NIV

First John 4:8 says God is love. The apostle Peter knew this, and he tells us in the Bible to love each other deeply because love covers a multitude of sins. In 1 Peter 4:9–11 he says, "Offer hospitality to one another without grumbling. Each of you should use whatever gift you have received to serve others, as faithful stewards of God's grace in its various forms. If anyone speaks, they should do so as one who speaks the very words of God. If anyone serves, they should do so with the strength God provides, so that in all things God may be praised through Jesus Christ." We could add be merciful, understanding, kind, caring, gentle, and every other characteristic that Jesus modeled for us while here on earth. Most of all, we should be forgiving.

When we serve one another and behave toward each other with Christlike love, we confront evil with righteousness and sin has nowhere to go. We cover it and smother it, allowing the light of Christ's love to shine brightly.

Lord God, let Your love radiate through me.
Inspire me to love others the way You love me. Amen.

DIFFERENT PATHS, SAME DESTINATION

Show me Your ways, O Lord. Teach me Your paths.

PSALM 25:4 NLV

How many of these coffee drinks have you tried?

Coffee with cream and sugar
Café au lait
Iced coffee
Cold brew
Espresso
Americano
Latte
Cappuccino
Mocha
Flat white
Macchiato
Breve
Irish coffee
Affogato
Frappé
Vienna coffee

Perhaps all are familiar to you, or maybe you wondered what some were and looked them up. There are many varieties, and each tastes different, but all have one thing in common: coffee.

Our spiritual journeys are as many and as varied as coffee drinks, but all have Jesus in common. He leads us down different paths with salvation as the destination. Many Christians have interesting, surprising, or even shocking stories of what led them to invite Jesus into their hearts. Everyone has a story of how they came to know Him. Sharing our stories inspires others on their path to salvation. Who led you to Jesus? Did someone's story inspire you?

Dear Jesus, thank You for those who lead us to Your gift of forgiveness of sin and eternal life in heaven. Amen.

COFFEE CULTURE

There is no difference between the Jews and the people who are not Jews. They are all the same to the Lord. And He is Lord over all of them. He gives of His greatness to all who call on Him for help.

ROMANS 10:12 NLV

Different cultures have their own traditions of enjoying coffee. In America, people begin the day with black coffee, doctor it with cream and sugar, or enjoy a specialty coffee from a coffee shop. In Italy, espresso is the go-to morning drink, strong and sipped from tiny cups. Morning coffee in France is café au lait. And in Ethiopia, coffee is a ceremony in which beans are roasted, ground, cooked in a kettle, and the coffee served in handleless cups. Some coffee aficionados travel the world and delight in meeting new people and sharing the knowledge, history, and taste of their coffees.

The people on God's earth are a beautiful combination of varying races, ethnicities, and nationalities. God created them all. He doesn't judge by skin color, customs, or how they like their coffee. In His eyes, everyone is equal, and He invites all to sit at Jesus' table and share in the cup of salvation.

Dear Jesus, sit at my table. Let's talk awhile as I enjoy my morning coffee. Amen.

HOW COULD HE?

For Christ is not only God-like. He is God in human flesh.
COLOSSIANS 2:9 NLV

"How could a loving father allow his son to die in such a way?" Some view Christ's crucifixion from a purely human point of view, comparing God to a human father who allowed His Son to die in the cruelest and most painful way. But God is not a human father. Beyond our comprehension, God and Jesus exist simultaneously as Father and Son. If we view Jesus' crucifixion from that perspective, things change.

Christ's crucifixion was not God proving His power over humans by inflicting terrible pain and suffering on His human Son. Instead, it was God in the flesh, enduring the pain and suffering that we humans inflict on Him when we sin. Would you die for your child? God took the punishment that we, as His children, deserved for our sins. Because He loves us, God sacrificed a part of Himself so we can live forever.

In Luke 23:34 (KJV), Jesus spoke from the cross, saying, "Father, forgive them; for they know not what they do." We are the "they" in that sentence. Isn't it wonderful to know we're forgiven?

Lord Jesus, I'm sorry for the times I've hurt You. Thank You for enduring the pain and suffering and forgiving me for my sins. Amen.

ONE IN A MILLION?

I will give thanks to You, for the greatness of the way I was made brings fear. Your works are great and my soul knows it very well.

PSALM 139:14 NLV

Did you know that about one septillion snowflakes fall during an average winter? To put it in perspective, a septillion is equal to a trillion trillion. That's a lot of snowflakes! Now consider that no two snowflakes are exactly alike. A septillion snowflakes, no two alike, each brilliantly designed by our Creator.

Like snowflakes, we humans are unique and complex. Each of us is shaped for God's purpose. He gives us not only one-of-a-kind DNA but unique creative gifts (1 Corinthians 7:7), reasons for existence (Ephesians 1:11), abilities (2 Corinthians 3:5), personalities (1 Samuel 16:7), and experiences (Romans 8:28). So if you see snowflakes spilling from the sky, remember that you are not all that different from those matchless, tiny masses of ice. In God's eyes, you are small, and yet you are a perfect and indispensable part of His great and mighty plan.

You aren't one in a million or even a septillion—you are unique to every person who has ever existed and ever will. Now fathom that!

Lord God, You made me unique and wonderful. Now please help me to be the best I can be. Amen.

SPRING

The winter is past; the rains are over and gone. Flowers appear on the earth; the season of singing has come, the cooing of doves is heard in our land.

Song of Songs 2:11–12 NIV

Spring filled the air. A gentle breeze carried the sweet scent of cherry blossoms, and vivid sunlight shone in the cloudless blue sky. It was a day of tender reflection. Sue was in hospice care. Her days numbered, she quietly contemplated the season. "I've always loved spring," she said. "God is good. He knows exactly how to give us a fresh start." She was about to enter her own personal spring, a season unlike any here on earth. A fresh start in heaven.

Fresh starts don't always come with gentle breezes and bright sunshine. Sometimes, they come veiled in storm clouds. Winter comes hitting hard and lingers dark. But we know that spring will eventually come. It always does. It has since the beginning because that is God's plan.

Maybe today you are waiting for a veil of storm clouds to lift and for God to reveal your new beginning. Have faith. Spring will come again. It might be different from any spring you have ever known. But spring *will* come. He guarantees it.

Lord, please clear this veil of clouds and guide me back to spring. Amen.

HEAVENLY COLORS

"But I will rebuild you with turquoise stones,
and I will build your foundations with sapphires."

ISAIAH 54:11 NCV

Were you a kid who loved opening a big box of crayons and seeing so many colors? Some people who have had near-death experiences recall colors in heaven so unique words couldn't describe them. Revelation 21:19–21 gives us a glimpse of heaven's shining city:

> *"The foundation stones of the city walls were decorated with every kind of jewel. The first foundation was jasper, the second was sapphire, the third was chalcedony, the fourth was emerald, the fifth was onyx, the sixth was carnelian, the seventh was chrysolite, the eighth was beryl, the ninth was topaz, the tenth was chrysoprase, the eleventh was jacinth, and the twelfth was amethyst. The twelve gates were twelve pearls, each gate having been made from a single pearl. And the street of the city was made of pure gold as clear as glass."*

Beyond the crayon box is an infinite number of colors. Gem colors. Dazzling colors. Vivid colors. Colors so stunning and so indescribable that only God can speak their names. That's what we can look forward to in heaven.

Lord God, if heaven exceeds the beauty of earth, how lovely it must be. How wonderful are Your works. Amen.

YOUTHFUL THOUGHTS

Remember also your Maker while you are young.

ECCLESIASTES 12:1 NLV

Young adults often wonder, *Who am I? Where am I going? Who do I want to be? Why are relationships hard? Why is life tough?* Youthful thoughts blend wonder with worry. It's like riding a fast train that races in one direction while glimpses of other trains whiz by in the opposite direction, appearing as fleeting shadows and flashes of light.

The book of Ecclesiastes begins with a man pondering youthful questions. Nothing in his world gives him a sense of meaning or peace. But by the end of the book, the man has become transformed and settled, realizing that life rushes by and happiness doesn't come from worldly things. It comes from focusing on God, trusting His plan, and accepting His will.

Maybe you are still in the youthful stage of learning. Focus on God, your teacher. Follow Him and trust Him. Life is an amazing journey that can lead to wisdom and peace. Time passes quickly and you'll reach your destination sooner than you think. Your youthful days of analyzing thoughts and reaching for dreams will soon give way to a settled, wise maturity.

Dear Jesus, help me to focus only on what's important: following You, learning from You, trusting You, and accepting Your will. Amen.

COME RAIN OR SHINE

He covers the heavens with clouds. He gives rain for the earth. He makes grass grow on the mountains.

PSALM 147:8 NLV

We listen to meteorologists to find out the temperature and if the sun will shine tomorrow. Then we tune out their words. That changes, though, when dark clouds appear and warning sirens wail. Then we listen to the meteorologist's every word. We want to know where the storm is now, when it will hit us, and how bad it will be. Meteorologists can answer those questions and tell us how to protect ourselves.

Our relationship with the Lord is much like our relationship with the weather forecaster. On good days, we routinely check in with God through Bible reading and prayer, and then we check out. On bad days, we plead for more information. "Tell me that the storm won't hit me. If it does hit me, tell me that it won't be bad. If it is bad, then save me."

God wants us to tune in and listen to Him every day, both good and bad. When we listen carefully in all kinds of weather, we know we'll be safe when it storms.

Lord God, on good days and bad I will seek You and listen to Your every word. Amen.

DESIRING GOD

My soul has a desire for You in the night.
Yes, my spirit within me looks for You in the morning.
ISAIAH 26:9 NLV

Diane had just bought her first house, and after years of apartment living, she was eager to plant a vegetable garden. At the garden center, she purchased starter plants of kale, several kinds of lettuce, peppers, cucumbers, and tomatoes. After carefully preparing the soil, she planted her garden, stood back, and admired her work.

"Did you protect the plants from rabbits?" asked her dad when she spoke with him on the phone.

"There aren't any rabbits around here," Diane said.

"There will be," he responded.

He was right! Within days, Diane noticed that her plants were nothing but stubble. She did her best to protect what was left, but the rabbits still ate them all.

There is one thing we can admire about rabbits: their tenacity. They yearn for what they know is good for them, and they stop at nothing to get it. That's how we should be in our desire for God. Nothing should stop us from seeking Him and drawing nourishment from His Word. Ask Him today to strengthen your longing for Him.

Dear Jesus, please deepen my desire for You and Your Word. Beckon me nearer to You. Amen.

A PLACE FOR YOU

"All of your people will do what is right. . . .
They are the plant I have planted, the work
of my own hands to show my greatness."
ISAIAH 60:21 NCV

God has a plan for His people here on earth and also a place. Some find themselves firmly planted from the day they are born and stay in their hometowns all their lives. Others God picks up and transplants where He wants them. Wherever that place, we know it when we get there because it feels right. It feels like home.

Even if you haven't found your place here on earth, Jesus has planned and prepared a place for you in heaven. In John 14:3 He says, "After I go and prepare a place for you, I will come back and take you to be with me so that you may be where I am."

Do you feel at home where you are, or is somewhere tugging at your heart and beckoning you to come? Listen to your heart. Ask God where you should be. Wherever God takes you, He will care for you and provide for you there.

Jesus, wherever I live here on earth, I know
an even better place awaits me in heaven.
Thank You for getting it ready for me. Amen.

THE UGLY MUG

"Even if I say, 'I'll put all this behind me, I'll look on the bright side and force a smile,' all these troubles would still be like grit in my gut."
JOB 9:27 MSG

"Smile, Josh," his boss said. "It's a brand-new day, the sun is shining, and all is well with the world."

Josh forced a sarcastic smile.

We all know someone like him. He resembles one of those ugly-face pottery mugs, furrowed brow, sad eyes, pouty lips. People like Josh rarely smile, and if they do, it's fast and forced. They ask themselves, *Why should I smile? It won't wash my troubles away.* We avoid ugly mugs like Josh because they steal our sunshine.

Life isn't always sunshine and roses, but when we learn to look on the bright side, dreary days are easier to handle. A positive attitude makes us more resilient, reduces stress, and contributes to our overall wellness. It increases our motivation and helps us maintain good relationships.

What does your mug look like this morning? God is the potter. You are the clay. Ask Him to put a smile on your face as you enter this brand-new day.

Dear Jesus, I will start today with a smile on my face, and with Your help I'll keep it there all day long. Amen.

FILL YOUR CUP WITH GRATITUDE

Go into His gates giving thanks and into His holy place with praise. Give thanks to Him. Honor His name.

PSALM 100:4 NLV

At Thanksgiving, teachers ask children to write down what they are grateful for. Most answers are ordinary things like toys, pets, and candy. Others need an explanation, like the boy who wrote "gas" (hopefully the kind you put in cars!), the girl who was thankful for toilet paper, and the kindergartener who was grateful for the mermaid in the bathroom. When it comes to gratefulness, some children think outside the box. While their answers are amusing, they help us to look at gratefulness from an entirely different perspective.

Adults are grateful for family, health, financial security, and jobs. Those who believe in God have a long list of thanks that includes salvation, His provisions, and the wisdom that comes from His Word. All of these things are good and worthy of thanks. But we grown-ups often forget to thank God for little things like gas, toilet paper, and our ability to imagine mermaids.

Fill your cup with gratitude today. Think outside the box of things you haven't yet thanked God for. Add them to your praises and prayers.

Lord, thank You for cozy mysteries, popcorn on Saturday nights, morning coffee, and YOU. Amen.

NOW AND FOREVER

The Lord will watch over your coming and going, now and forever.
Psalm 121:8 NLV

There was a man who chronicled every minute of his life. He wrote in a journal every fifteen minutes, reporting about what he thought and observed, even little things like drinks of water. A solitary man, his study was packed with leather-bound journals, his entire adult life poured into thick stacks of yellowing pages. Why he did it isn't clear. He was obviously obsessed. It was important to him that someone knew he existed and that someone would remember him.[18]

Someone did remember—God. He knew this man even before He formed him in his mother's womb. God had already planned every minute of his life. There was no need to record it. God was there. He knew. God chronicles our lives in His Book of Life. He remembers every second of our days, the good things and the sinful. He forgives our sins and loves us so much that He sacrificed His own Son so we can live eternally in heaven. The Lord watches over everything we do now and forever. He remembers us, so let's remember Him. Make the Lord an integral part of each and every day.

Jesus, I will keep my thoughts fixed on You all day, every day. Amen.

[18] "'Way Ahead of His Time': Endowment Supports Cataloging of World's Longest Diary," *Washington State University*, September 26, 2024, https://libraries.wsu.edu/friends/2024/09/26/way-ahead-of-his-time-endowment-supports-cataloging-of-worlds-longest-diary/

UNTIL THE SHADOWS FLEE

Until the day breaks and the shadows flee, I will go to the mountain of myrrh and to the hill of incense.

SONG OF SONGS 4:6 NIV

Golden sunrays danced on the plane's wings. Patchwork fields passed slowly below, creating a quilt-like kaleidoscope of shifting colors. Foothills and fawn-colored mountains appeared. Beyond the crest of the highest mountain, its shadow was cast onto golden fields, a shadow so dark it looked like a patch of night settled onto the earth. The side of the mountain stayed shrouded in darkness, its secrets hidden from view. But beyond, the sun shone brightly as far as the eye could see.

God's kingdom is like that great mountain casting its shadow onto the earth. Hidden in its shadow lie all of God's secrets—why bad things happen to good people, where heaven is, and what our futures hold. Slowly, we walk through the shadow. We climb the mountain, scaling each steep wall and rugged cliff until, finally, we reach the mountaintop and see God's face. There, we stand with Him in the sunshine looking down at all the secrets revealed.

Lord God, guide me through my life with its beauty and hills and valleys. Then lead me through its shadow and up to the mountaintop where I'll meet You face-to-face. Amen.

MORE CAFFEINE

"But from there you will look for the Lord your God. And you will find Him if you look for Him with all your heart and soul."
DEUTERONOMY 4:29 NLV

Our busyness, responsibilities, and this noisy world make it difficult for us to find Jesus. We catch a glimpse of Him here and there, but finding Jesus requires looking for Him with all our hearts and souls.

Standard devotional time includes reading scripture, meditating on what you read, praying, and, if you've chosen this book, coffee! But you need to add some more "caffeine." Finding Jesus requires more than daily devotional time. It means motivating yourself to reach out to Him minute by minute, talking with Him throughout the day, seeking His advice, and seeing Him in the people and situations all around you.

You can find Jesus by listening to Christian radio and podcasts, reading Christian literature and devotionals, and keeping a prayer journal. Be creative in the ways you seek Him. Jesus wants a unique and everlasting relationship with you. If you look for Jesus, you will find Him.

Dear Jesus, I want us to have a special and eternal relationship. Every day, show me new and exciting ways I can connect with and grow nearer to You. Amen.

COFFEE AND JESUS

May the God of hope fill you with all joy and peace as you trust in him, so that you may overflow with hope by the power of the Holy Spirit.

ROMANS 15:13 NIV

Our daily life combines with Jesus like the perfect blend of coffee—rich and full-flavored with a balanced combination of sweetness and strength. Just as coffee's aroma fills the air, Jesus' presence in our lives can be a sweet fragrance that draws us to Him and each other. He will lead us into the future with new experiences, challenges, and opportunities.

When we begin our days with Jesus and coffee, our cups will never be empty; they will overflow with His love. Each day, He will fill our cups with joy and peace as we put our faith and trust in Him. Just as coffee can be customized to our individual tastes, Jesus meets us where we are with a personalized relationship that speaks directly to our hearts.

As you savor your coffee each day, make time to connect with Jesus. Listen to His voice and find rest in His loving presence.

Lord Jesus, may my relationship with you be just as vibrant and comforting as a good cup of coffee. May I be alert to your presence, attentive to your voice, and responsive to your leading. Amen.

SCRIPTURE INDEX

OLD TESTAMENT

Genesis
1:25 166
31:55 13
50:20–21 92

Exodus
12:26–27 161
14:14 102
17:12 130
33:11 33

Deuteronomy
4:29 187
8:7 48

Joshua
1:5 15
4:6 108

Judges
5:12 9
6:13 25

Ruth
1:16–17 67

1 Samuel
14:26 165

2 Samuel
22:21 53

2 Kings
23:3 160

Esther
4:14 57

Job
9:8–9 28
9:27 183
12:12 131
13:24 66
22:21 162
26:14 106

Psalms
4:1 34
4:8 118
16:11 151
19:1 155
19:14 18
23:3 72
23:4 132
25:4 173
27:13–14 97
34:4–5 37
34:8 10
42:11 116
45:13 54
46:5 74
73:26 88
83:1 128
91:11–12 168
92:15 110
94:19 150
94:23 21
100:4 184
102:7 119
104:24 65

107:2–3 ... 109
118:24 ... 143
119:30 ... 35
119:93 ... 134
119:105 ... 71
121:8 ... 185
126:3 ... 23
130:5–6 ... 136
131:2 ... 46
133:1 ... 121
139:14 ... 176
143:8 ... 7, 117
147:8 ... 180

Proverbs
3:5–6 ... 94
12:25 ... 90
16:24 ... 129
16:32 ... 85
17:22 ... 167
18:13 ... 153
22:3 ... 81
24:3–4 ... 125
25:19 ... 36
26:22 ... 111
27:12 ... 61
31:25 ... 76
31:26 ... 78
31:29 ... 77

Ecclesiastes
3:19, 21 ... 105
4:9 ... 157
12:1 ... 179

Song of Songs
2:11–12 ... 177
4:6 ... 186

Isaiah
1:18 ... 123
6:8 ... 49
26:9 ... 181
30:21 ... 127
41:10 ... 133
43:2–3 ... 59
45:3 ... 144
51:12 ... 39
54:11 ... 178
58:11 ... 52
60:21 ... 182

Jeremiah
10:23 ... 159
17:7–8 ... 75
29:11 ... 17
33:3 ... 140
50:6 ... 38

Lamentations
3:22–23 ... 11

Joel
2:13 ... 80

Micah
5:2 ... 152
7:8 ... 26

Habakkuk
3:19 ... 169

NEW TESTAMENT

Matthew
5:9 51
10:19–20 58
10:29 107
11:30 55
18:20 73
19:14 95
22:37–39 20
24:6 103
25:23 135
26:33 101

Luke
1:37 138
6:38 14
10:41–42 139
11:1 64
11:11, 13 82
17:9–10 148
18:13 170
22:42 63
23:34 93

John
6:2 164
7:24 68
15:16 45
21:25 98

Acts
20:35 62

Romans
4:13 158
5:3 86
8:28 27
10:12 174
12:12 24
14:1 31
15:13 188

1 Corinthians
2:2 70
4:3 69
13:2 84
13:12 120

2 Corinthians
5:17 96
5:20 145
12:9 163
12:10 29

Galatians
1:10 147
5:22–23 44
6:4 156

Ephesians
2:8–9 114
3:12 141
3:18 99
3:20 47
4:29 19
6:5 124

Philippians
1:3 60
2:10–11 30

3:12.....................113
4:6–7 91
4:8.........................12
4:13.......................32

Colossians

1:29.....................149
2:9.......................175
3:23–24...................79

1 Thessalonians

5:18.......................56

2 Timothy

2:7.......................137
2:24.....................154
3:16–17...................42
4:7.........................89

Titus

2:4.......................122

Philemon

1:7.......................115

Hebrews

4:16.......................22
10:24–25 40
13:2.......................41
13:8.....................126

James

2:14.......................43

1 Peter

3:4.......................104
4:8.......................172
4:10.....................146

1 John

1:8, 10 171
2:16–17...................16
3:1.........................50
3:18.......................83
4:8.........................87
4:12.....................100

3 John

10 112

Revelation

3:20.....................142